WORKBOOK
WITH EBOOK

Vicki Anderson and Lynn Durrant

Shaftesbury Road, Cambridge CB2 8EA, United Kingdom

One Liberty Plaza, 20th Floor, New York, NY 10006, USA

477 Williamstown Road, Port Melbourne, VIC 3207, Australia

314–321, 3rd Floor, Plot 3, Splendor Forum, Jasola District Centre, New Delhi – 110025, India

103 Penang Road, #05-06/07, Visioncrest Commercial, Singapore 238467

Avenida Paulista, 807 conjunto 2315, 01311–915, São Paulo, Brazil

Torre de los Parques, Colonia Tlacoquemécatl del Valle, Mexico City, cp 03200, Mexico

Cambridge University Press & Assessment is a department of the University of Cambridge.

We share the University's mission to contribute to society through the pursuit of education, learning and research at the highest international levels of excellence.

www.cambridge.org
Information on this title: www.cambridge.org/9781009043014

First published 2021

20 19 18 17 16 15 14 13 12 11 10 9 8

Printed in Great Britain by Ashford Colour Press Ltd.

A catalogue record for this publication is available from the British Library

ISBN 978-1-009-04301-4 Shape It! Workbook with eBook Level 1
ISBN 978-1-009-04351-9 Own it! Workbook with eBook Level 1

Additional resources for this publication at www.cambridge.org/shapeit

CONTENTS

STARTER
Welcome!

VOCABULARY AND READING
Months, Cardinal and Ordinal Numbers, and Colors

1 ⭐ **Complete the sentences with the months in the box and ordinal numbers.**

> April   August   February   ~~January~~
> June   March   November   October

1 _____January_____ is the first month.
2 _____ is the _____ month.
3 _____ is the third month.
4 _____ is the _____ month.
5 May is the _____ month.
6 _____ is the sixth month.
7 July is the _____ month.
8 _____ is the _____ month.
9 September is the _____ month.
10 _____ is the tenth month.
11 _____ is the _____ month.
12 December is the _____ month.

2 ⭐⭐ **Complete the crossword with seven more colors.**

ACROSS →
2 three letters
3 four letters
4 six letters
7 five letters
8 five letters

DOWN ↓
1 five letters
5 six letters
6 four letters

```
        ¹G
       ²R _ _
 ³_ _ _ E
        E    ⁵      ⁶
 ⁴_ _ _ N
       ⁷B L A C K
              ⁸_ _ _ _ _
```

An Online Profile

3 ⭐⭐ **Read about Dasha and Carlos. Where are their friends from?**

| Home | **Profile** | Photos | Events |

INTERNATIONAL STUDENT PROFILE DAY!

Hello! My name's Dasha. I'm from Warsaw in Poland. I'm 12. How old are you? In this photo, I'm with my two best friends. Polina is Polish, but Marta isn't Polish. She's Brazilian. My favorite color is green. What's your favorite color? My birthday is April 10. When's your birthday? My dream is to be a doctor! What's your dream? Write soon!

Hi, Dasha! I'm Carlos. I'm Mexican, from Mexico City. I'm 11. In this photo, I'm with my best friends. They're not Mexican. Yusuf is from Turkey, and David is from England. My favorite color is blue. It's June 5 tomorrow, and it's my birthday! My dream is to be a singer! Who's your favorite singer?

Let me know!

4 **Read the profiles again and complete the chart.**

Name	Birthday	Favorite Color	Dream
Dasha	April 10	green	¹ _doctor_
² _____	³ _____	⁴ _____	singer

5 ⭐⭐ **Circle the correct answers.**

1 Dasha is from *China* / *Poland*.
2 Her birthday is in the *fourth* / *seventh* month of the year.
3 Carlos is from *Turkey* / *Mexico*.
4 His birthday is in the *sixth* / *twelfth* month of the year.
5 *David* / *Carlos* is 12 tomorrow.

GRAMMAR IN ACTION AND VOCABULARY

Subject Pronouns and Possessive Adjectives

1 ⭐ **Complete the chart with the subject pronouns in the box.**

> it   they   we   ~~you~~

Singular	Plural
I	³_____
¹___you___	you
he / she / ²_____	⁴_____

2 ⭐ **Write the subject pronoun.**

1 Dasha ____she____
2 photos _____
3 school _____
4 Carlos _____
5 Polina and Marta _____
6 Yusuf and I _____

3 ⭐ **Which plural pronoun can we use for objects and people?**

_____

4 ⭐ **Complete the sentences with the possessive adjectives in the box.**

> her   his   its   my   our   ~~their~~   your

1 Yusuf and Carlos are at school. They're in ____their____ classroom.
2 He's from Poland. _____ name's Max.
3 I'm 12 years old, and _____ best friend, Alba, is 11.
4 We're from China. _____ nationality is Chinese.
5 You're 13. _____ birthday is in April.
6 My teacher is Maria. _____ birthday is in August.
7 This school is nice. _____ classrooms are big!

Verb *To Be*

5 ⭐⭐ **Complete the profile with the correct form of *to be*.**

My name ¹___is___ Sofía. I ²_____ from Chile. My best friend ³_____ Ana. She ⁴_____ (not) from Chile. She ⁵_____ from Brazil. My favorite singer ⁶_____ Lorde. My favorite songs ⁷_____ *Green Light* and *Royals*. They ⁸_____ incredible!

Question Words

6 ⭐ **Match questions 1–5 with answers a–e.**

1 Where are you from? [c]
2 How old are you? [ ]
3 When's your birthday? [ ]
4 Who's your best friend? [ ]
5 What's your favorite number? [ ]

a May 10.   d Alba.
b It's 15.   e I'm 11.
c ~~I'm from Miami.~~

Classroom Objects

7 ⭐ **Look at the pictures. (Circle) the correct words.**

1 It's a *board* / (*calculator*).   4 They're *pens* / *pencils*.
2 They're *chairs* / *desks*.   5 It's a *pen* / *pencil*.
3 It's a *window* / *door*.   6 They're *rulers* / *notebooks*.

LISTENING AND GRAMMAR IN ACTION
An Introduction

🎧 **1** ⭐ **Listen and (circle) the correct answer.**
S.01

Elena's from *Spain / Brazil.*

🎧 **2** ⭐ **Listen again. Number the instructions in the order you hear them (1–4).**
S.01

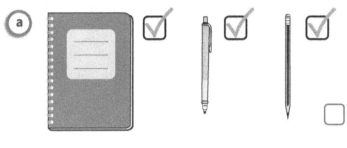

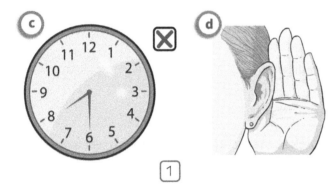

🎧 **3** ⭐⭐ **Listen again. Are the sentences *T* (true) or *F* (false)?**
S.01

1 This is Elena's first day at school.   T
2 She's from the capital of Brazil.   ___
3 She's the only student from Brazil in her class.   ___
4 Her notebook is on her desk.   ___
5 Her pens and pencils are in her bag.   ___
6 The ruler on the desk is hers.   ___

Whose + Possessive Pronouns

4 ⭐⭐ **Complete the sentences with the correct possessive pronouns.**

1 Whose dictionaries are these?
  They're their dictionaries. They're ____theirs____ .
2 Whose ruler is this?
  It's my ruler. It's _____ .
3 Whose books are these?
  They're our books. They're _____ .
4 Whose poster is that?
  It's her poster. It's _____ .
5 Whose chairs are those?
  They're your chairs. They're _____ .
6 Whose calculator is this?
  It's his calculator. It's _____ .

Imperatives

5 ⭐⭐ **Put the words in the correct order to make sentences.**

1 write / Don't / notebook / my / in
  Don't write in my notebook.
2 board / the / Write / the / words / on
  _____
3 late / Don't / for / be / class
  _____
4 teacher / to / Listen / the
  _____
5 eat / in / class / Don't
  _____
6 book / your / Close
  _____

6 ⭐⭐⭐ **Write two more instructions for your class.**

_____
_____
_____
_____
_____

WRITING
An Informal Letter

1 ⭐ **Read Jenny's letter. Who is from Australia?**

20 Marsh Street
Newark, NJ 07114

October 20

Dear Lucy,

1 My name is Jenny Watts, and I'm 12. I'm from Newark, New Jersey in the United States.

2 My school is great. The classroom is green, orange, and white. It's very nice, with a lot of posters on the walls. Our teacher is friendly, and I'm happy in my new class.

3 My best friend isn't in my class. She goes to a different school. She isn't American like me. She's Australian. Her name is Sarah.

4 My favorite object is my new red and blue notebook. My favorite number is five – my birthday is May 5! My dream is to be a famous singer like you!

Sincerely,

Jenny

2 ⭐ **Read the letter again. Match topics a–d with paragraphs 1–4.**

a favorite object, number, birthday, and dream ☐

b name, age, and where she's from ☐ 1

c best friend and nationality ☐

d school and class ☐

3 ⭐ **Match phrases 1–3 with functions a–c.**

1 Sincerely, ☐

2 Our teacher is friendly, <u>and</u> I'm happy in my new class. ☐

3 Dear Lucy, ☐

a to start a letter

b to end a letter

c to join two ideas in one sentence

PLAN

4 ⭐⭐ **Write an informal letter. Decide what information to include in each paragraph. Use the information in Exercise 2 to help you.**

WRITE

5 ⭐⭐⭐ **Write your letter. Remember to include four paragraphs, the address and date, and expressions from the *Useful Language* box (see Student's Book, p9).**

CHECK

6 **Do you ...**
- introduce yourself and give your name, age, and nationality?
- use *and* to join ideas?
- say what your dream is?

1 What is your family like?

Carlos — Maria

Marta — David   Javier — Lucía

Lucas   Ana (Me!)   Pedro   Julia

VOCABULARY
Family Members

1 ☆ Find 14 more words for family in the word search. Look at the words in Exercise 2 to help you.

W	G	N	E	P	H	E	W	G	S	O	N
B	R	O	T	H	E	R	D	F	T	S	E
R	A	D	G	U	J	I	N	K	M	W	K
A	N	U	T	S	S	K	J	I	E	A	Y
V	D	W	H	B	C	U	N	C	L	E	D
G	M	O	M	A	K	E	H	K	M	Y	A
D	A	T	S	N	H	D	A	D	W	D	U
G	R	A	N	D	P	A	E	Q	I	F	G
R	G	U	W	J	O	P	R	T	F	Q	H
B	D	N	I	E	C	E	I	M	E	P	T
F	G	T	K	H	O	S	N	G	X	V	E
C	O	U	S	I	N	S	I	S	T	E	R

2 ☆ Match 1–8 with a–h to make family word pairs.

1 brother   [f]
2 nephew   ☐
3 husband   ☐
4 grandpa   ☐
5 uncle   ☐
6 dad   ☐
7 son   ☐
8 grandson   ☐

a mom
b wife
c daughter
d aunt
e grandma
f ~~sister~~
g granddaughter
h niece

3 ☆ Which family word in Exercise 1 can be male or female? _____

4 ☆☆ Look at Ana's family tree. Complete her sentences with the correct family words.

1 Carlos is my ___grandpa___ and María is my _____ .

2 Marta is my _____ and David is my _____ .

3 Javier is my _____ and Lucía is my _____ .

4 Lucas is my _____ .

5 Pedro and Julia are my _____ .

5 ☆☆ (Circle) the correct answer to complete the riddle.

GUS	Hi! I'm Gus, and my sisters are April, May, and June. This is my mom.
MOM	Hi! I'm a mom with four children. My daughters are April, May, and June, and this is my son. His name is _____ .

a July   b September   c Gus

Explore It!

Guess the correct answer.

_____ is the most popular boy's name in the United States in the last 100 years.

a Robert   b John   c James

Find another interesting fact about names. Write a question and send it to a classmate in an email, or ask them in the next class.

READING
A Webpage

1 ⭐ **Read the webpage. What is it about? (Circle) the correct title.**

a A Big Family

b A Small Family

c A Family from Canada

2 ⭐⭐ **Read the webpage again and <u>underline</u> the words. Then check their meaning and complete the sentences.**

> dentist   everyone   fun   ~~neighbors~~   whole

1 Your house is next to mine. We're __neighbors__.

2 My aunt is a _____. Her job is to look at teeth!

3 A _____ day is 24 hours long.

4 My favorite day is Sunday with friends and family. It's _____!

5 This lesson is for all students. It's for _____.

3 ⭐⭐ **Read the webpage again. Are the sentences *T* (true) or *F* (false)?**

1 Tom is American.   T

2 His mom is a teacher.   ___

3 His family is typical because it's big.   ___

4 His cousins live on a different street.   ___

5 The family is together in the morning and evening.   ___

6 Tom is happy at home.   ___

4 ⭐⭐ **(Circle) the options that are true for you.**

1 My family is *big* / *small*.

2 My favorite time of day is the *morning* / *evening*.

3 My neighbors *are* / *aren't* at my birthday parties.

Tom is from Durham, North Carolina, in the United States. He's seven years old today! His parents' names are Helen and Richard. His mom is a dentist, and his dad is a middle school teacher.

Tom's family isn't very typical. He has two brothers and three sisters, and his grandma and grandpa live with them, too. Tom's aunt, uncle, and four cousins have a house in front of his. The whole family lives on the same street!

Tom's favorite times are the morning and the evening. That's when his family is all together for breakfast and dinner – there are ten people around the table!

Birthdays in Tom's family are fun, too. They have a birthday party every month! Today, everyone is at Tom's party: his family, his friends, and his neighbors.

Is Tom happy in his big family? Yes, he has good friends at school, and a lot of brothers, sisters, and cousins at home!

GRAMMAR IN ACTION
To Have: Affirmative and Negative

1 ⭐ (Circle) **the correct options.**

1 Richard and Helen (have) / *has* six children.
2 My grandma *have* / *has* a red car.
3 I *don't* / *doesn't* have a big family.
4 My dad *don't* / *doesn't* have any cousins.
5 My friend's parents *have* / *has* a big house.
6 Uncle Bill *don't* / *doesn't* have any children.

2 ⭐⭐ **Complete the text with the correct form of *to have*.**

My name is Claudia. I'm from Mexico, but I live in Australia with my family. I ¹ _____have_____ a big family. I ² _____ five brothers and two sisters. My parents ³ _____ a big house – it's perfect for a big family! My dad's name is Javier. He ⁴ _____ a lot of brothers and sisters, too. My mom is named Sandra. She ⁵ _____ a brother in Mexico – that's my Uncle Sergio. I ⁶ _____ any aunts or uncles in Australia. They're all in different countries. My best friend, Helen, is Australian. She ⁷ _____ any brothers or sisters. It's only her! She ⁸ _____ a small family, but they're really fun! 😊

3 ⭐⭐ **Write the words in the correct order to make sentences. Then match them with pictures a–e.**

1 bike / I / have / a / don't
I don't have a bike. ⌷b⌷

2 My / have / grandpa / doesn't / a / cell phone
_____ ☐

3 home / We / pets / at / four / have
_____ ☐

4 best friends / at / school / two / I / have
_____ ☐

5 My / two / has / boards / classroom
_____ ☐

ⓐ   ⓑ   ⓒ

ⓓ   ⓔ

Possessive *'s*

4 ⭐⭐ **Complete the sentences with the possessive *'s* and a family word.**

1 My mom _'s mom_____ is my grandma.
2 My cousin_____ is my uncle.
3 My dad_____ is my uncle.
4 My mom_____ is my aunt.
5 My brother_____ is my mom.
6 My dad_____ is my grandpa.

5 ⭐⭐⭐ **Find four facts about a famous family. Write four sentences about them. Use the correct form of *to have* and the possessive *'s*.**

Angelina Jolie has six children.
_____
_____
_____
_____

VOCABULARY AND LISTENING
Describing People

1 ⭐ Complete the list with the words in the box.

> blond   freckles   ~~gray~~   tall   wavy

Describing People

Eyes: [1] _gray_ , brown

Hairstyle: long, short, [2] _____

Hair color: [3] _____ , brown, gray, red

Height: [4] _____ , short

Other features: beard, [5] _____ , glasses, mustache

2 ⭐ Match the descriptions (1–4) with the photos (a–d).

1 glasses and long wavy hair
2 long hair and a beard
3 long blond hair
4 short brown hair and glasses

A Conversation

🎧 **3** ⭐⭐ Listen to the students talking about their families. Write *Paul's family, Emma's family, Jon's family,* or *Sue's family* under the correct pictures.
1.01

🎧 **4** ⭐⭐ Listen again. Circle the correct answers.
1.01
1 Paul has *four* / *five* brothers and sisters.
2 Paul *has* / *doesn't have* blond hair.
3 Emma's sister *has* / *doesn't have* freckles.
4 Emma has a friend with *long* / *short* hair.
5 Jon has *one brother* / *two brothers*.
6 Jon's mom *is* / *isn't* short.
7 Sue has *one tall brother* / *two tall brothers*.
8 *Sue's* / *Tony's* hair is red.

5 ⭐⭐⭐ Describe a friend. Include information from each category in Exercise 1.

My friend's name is Cindy. She has brown eyes and
long red hair.

_____

_____

_____

GRAMMAR IN ACTION
To Have: Questions

1 ⭐ Complete the chart with *have, has, do, does, don't,* or *doesn't.*

[1] Do you _have_ any cousins?	Yes, I [2] _____.	No, I [3] _____.
[4] _____ they have red hair?	Yes, they [5] _____.	No, they [6] _____.
Does she [7] _____ green eyes?	Yes, she [8] _____.	No, she [9] _____.
How many sisters [10] _____ he have?	He [11] _____ two sisters.	

2 ⭐ Complete the questions with the correct form of *to have*. Then match them with answers a–f.

1 ___Do___ you ___have___ any brothers and sisters? [b]
2 _____ your niece _____ brown hair? ☐
3 _____ you and your family _____ a big house? ☐
4 _____ your dad _____ a beard? ☐
5 _____ your parents _____ a car? ☐
6 _____ your house _____ a lot of rooms? ☐

a No, he doesn't.
b ~~No, I don't.~~
c Yes, they do.
d Yes, she does.
e Yes, it does.
f No, we don't.

3 ⭐⭐ Complete the conversation with the correct form of *to have* and the words in parentheses.

BETH Hi, Jan. [1] *Do you have* (you) a lot of homework?

JAN No, I [2] _____.

BETH Good. I have some questions about a school project.
[3] _____ (you) any brothers and sisters?

JAN Yes, I [4] _____. I have two brothers. They're twins.

BETH [5] _____ (they) green eyes like you?

JAN Yes, they [6] _____!

BETH Cool! And [7] _____ (your mom) brown hair like you?

JAN No, she [8] _____. She has blond hair.

4 ⭐⭐⭐ Read the answers from an interview with a famous actor. Write questions with *to have*. Use *How many* when necessary.

1 Do you have a big house? _____
   Yes, I do. My house is very big.

2 _____ ?
   Yes, we have five children, including twins!

3 _____ ?
   We have three boys and two girls.

4 _____ ?
   My wife has a horse, and the children have two rabbits.

5 _____ ?
   Yes, I do. I have two Oscars!

WRITING
An Informal Email

1 ⭐ **Look at the photos and read the email. Which photo is of Kylie and Kate? Mark (✓) the correct photo.**

TO: Ed

FROM: Kate

Hi Ed,

1 How are things? I'm in a new school, and I have a new friend. This email is about her.

2 I have a lot of friends in my class, but one girl 1('s)/ 've my best friend. Her name 2're / 's Kylie. We say we 3're / 've twins – we look the same! We have brown hair and green eyes, and we have the same birthday! It 4's / 're funny! 😄 And we both have a little brother. My brother 5're / 's ten and Kylie's brother 6's / 're nine.

3 The photo is of Kylie and me playing basketball. Kylie's a lot of fun and a great friend. 😊

4 Do you have good friends at your new school? Do you have a best friend? Email me soon!

That's all for now,

Kate

2 ⭐⭐ **Circle the correct contractions in the email.**

3 ⭐⭐ **Read the email again. Are the sentences *T* (true) or *F* (false)?**

1 Kate and Kylie are best friends.   T
2 They are in different classes.   ___
3 Their birthdays are on the same day.   ___
4 Kate doesn't have brown hair.   ___
5 Kylie doesn't have green eyes.   ___
6 They both have a little brother.   ___
7 Kate's brother is ten.   ___

4 ⭐⭐ **Match topics a–d with paragraphs 1–4 in the email.**

a extra information about a photo   `3`
b description of a new friend at school   ☐
c introduction and reason for writing   ☐
d Kate's questions for Ed   ☐

PLAN

5 ⭐⭐ **Write an informal email to a friend about a new school friend. Make notes about these things:**

your friend's name and age

_____

your friend's physical description and family

6 **Decide what information to include in each paragraph. Use the information in Exercise 4 to help you.**

WRITE

7 ⭐⭐⭐ **Remember to include four paragraphs, the verbs *to be* and *to have*, and expressions from the *Useful Language* box (see Student's Book, p17).**

CHECK

8 **Do you ...**
- use expressions to start and end your email?
- give information about your friend in the second paragraph?
- use information from a photo in the third paragraph?
- ask questions in the last paragraph?

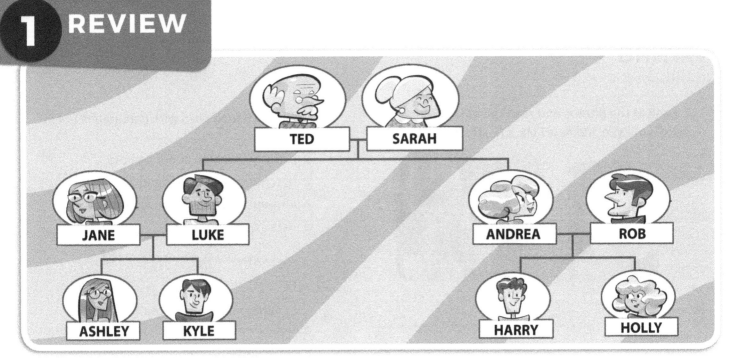

VOCABULARY

1 Look at the family tree. Are the sentences *T* (true) or *F* (false)? Correct the false sentences.

1 Ashley is Kyle's brother. ___
_____

2 Jane is Luke's sister. ___
_____

3 Ted is Ashley's grandpa. ___
_____

4 Luke is Andrea's cousin. ___
_____

5 Jane is Kyle's mom. ___
_____

6 Luke is Jane's brother. ___
_____

7 Kyle and Harry are Ted's grandsons. ___
_____

8 Sarah is Luke's and Andrea's grandmother. ___
_____

9 Rob is Ashley and Kyle's dad. ___
_____

10 Holly is Jane's and Luke's niece. ___
_____

2 (Circle) the word that doesn't fit.

1 mustache / beard / (tall)   4 blue / green / short
2 wavy / glasses / short   5 long / blond / red
3 blond / freckles / brown   6 brown / tall / wavy

GRAMMAR IN ACTION

3 (Circle) the correct options.

Victor and Anna ¹*has / have* a big house. It ²*has / have* a big yard and seven rooms. They ³*has / have* one daughter named Siena. They ⁴*don't have / have* any sons. Anna and Siena ⁵*has / have* blond hair. Anna ⁶*has / have* blue eyes, and Siena ⁷*has / have* brown eyes. Victor ⁸*has / have* three sports cars. They're his favorite! Anna ⁹*don't have / doesn't have* a sports car, but she ¹⁰*has / have* a mobile home!

4 Write questions with the correct form of *to have*. Use *How many* when necessary. Then look at Exercise 3 on page 14 and answer the questions.

1 Victor and Anna / a big yard?

_____

2 rooms / their house?

_____

3 they / sons?

_____

4 Siena / blond hair?

_____

5 sports cars / Victor?

_____

6 Anna / mobile home?

_____

CUMULATIVE GRAMMAR

5 Match questions 1–8 with answers a–h.

1 Do your grandparents have a big yard? ☐
2 What do we have for homework? ☐
3 How many cousins do you have? ☐
4 Do you have an English dictionary? ☐
5 Does your dad have a beard? ☐
6 When do we have our exam? ☐
7 Is that Amalia's baby brother? ☐
8 Wow! How many books do your parents have? ☐

a I have four.
b Yes, they do. It's my favorite place!
c I don't know. I think they have hundreds!
d No, he doesn't! But he has a mustache.
e Yes, I do.
f We have the exercises on page 14.
g No! It's her nephew. He's her sister's baby.
h I'm not sure. I think it's in November.

VOCABULARY
Daily Routines

1 ⭐ **Complete the crossword. Use the clues.**

ACROSS →

2 You pack your ___bag___ with your books for school.

5 I have _____ with my family. We have cereal.

7 After school, you check your _____ for messages.

10 In middle school, you do your _____ every evening.

11 First you wake up. Then you ___get up___ .

DOWN ↓

1 I _____ at seven o'clock, but I get up at 7:15.

3 At night, you _____ and sleep.

4 In the morning, I ___get dressed___ . I put on my school clothes.

5 I _____ my teeth after breakfast and before I go to bed.

6 After school, I go _____ on the bus.

8 I go to _____ from Monday to Friday, but not on the weekend!

9 I take a _____ when I get up and after sports.

2 ⭐ **Complete the daily routines with the verbs in the box.**

> brush   check   do   get (x2)
> go (x3)   have   pack   take   wake

1 ___get___ up   7 _____ to school

2 _____ dressed   8 _____ my phone

3 _____ my teeth 9 _____ to bed

4 _____ breakfast 10 _____ up

5 _____ home   11 _____ a shower

6 _____ my bag   12 _____ my homework

3 ⭐⭐ **Complete the text with the correct form of the phrases from Exercise 2.**

This is my ideal school day. I [1] ___wake up___ at nine o'clock, and I [2] _____ for messages. I [3] _____ at 9:15, I take a shower, and I [4] _____ . These are my favorite clothes. Then I [5] _____ (cereal). At ten o'clock, I brush my teeth, I [6] _____ with my books, and I [7] _____ on the bus. I have three classes, and I go home to have lunch. I don't have any homework! After dinner, I check my phone again and I [8] _____ .

4 ⭐⭐⭐ **Write about your ideal school day. Use Exercise 3 to help you.**

This is my ideal school day. I …

_____

_____

_____

Explore It! 🖱

Guess the correct answer.

People in the United States *get dressed / take a shower* in eight minutes.

Find another interesting fact about daily routines in your country. Write a question and send it to a classmate in an email, or ask them in the next class.

READING
A Profile

1 ⭐ **Read the profile. Is this sentence *T* (true) or *F* (false)?**

Dylan has 25 hours of classes a week. _____

A Day in the Life of a
Child Actor

Dylan Roberts is 14, and he's a child actor. He makes movies and doesn't go to school. He always has classes with special teachers called on-set teachers. Child actors usually have 15 hours of classes a week (schools have 25), but it isn't easy! Dylan often has a lot of work to do.

2 ⭐⭐ **Read the profile again and <u>underline</u> these words. Then check their meaning in a dictionary and complete the sentences.**

> break   busy   filming
> ~~makeup~~   on-set teacher

1 Here's the green ___makeup___ for your eyes.
2 After three classes, we have a _____ to have lunch.
3 All the actors are ready for _____ today.
4 I have an _____ for extra English classes.
5 Our weekends are very _____ with a lot of things to do!

3 ⭐⭐ **Read the profile again. Ⓒircle the correct answer.**

1 Dylan is a child actor. He *goes* / *doesn't go* to school.
2 Dylan's special teacher is an *on-set teacher* / *actor*.
3 A child actor *has* / *doesn't have* a lot of work to do.
4 Dylan has breakfast at *home* / *work*.
5 Dylan's first classes are *before* / *after* filming.
6 He doesn't have any *homework* / *breaks*.

4 ⭐⭐ **What's your opinion? Read the statements and write *Yes* or *No*.**

1 It's easy to be a child actor. _____
2 Fifteen hours of classes a week is a good idea. _____
3 Dylan's day is fun. _____
4 Not having homework is great. _____

Dylan talks about his typical day:

"I get up at six in the morning and get dressed. At 6:15, a car takes me to the movie set. I have breakfast at work, and then I practice the day's scenes for an hour. At 8:00, they do my hair and makeup. Filming starts at 9:00. Then, at 11:00, I have a break for half an hour. After that, I go to the teacher's room for classes. I don't have any homework. At 6:00 in the evening, I go home or to a hotel. I take a shower, have dinner, read my part of the movie for tomorrow, and go to bed. It's a busy day!"

GRAMMAR IN ACTION

Simple Present: Affirmative and Negative   **Adverbs of Frequency**

1 ⭐ (Circle) the correct options.

1 Dylan is a child actor and he *make* / (*makes*) movies.

2 Child actors *don't* / *doesn't* live at home when they are in a movie.

3 They *have* / *has* dinner in a hotel.

4 We *study* / *studies* English.

5 Maya *have* / *has* breakfast at school.

6 On-set teachers *teach* / *teaches* small classes.

2 ⭐ Write the third person singular of the simple present.

have	watch	meet	go
1 _has_	2	3	4

play	brush	do	hurry
5	6	7	8

3 ⭐⭐ Complete the text with the simple present form of the verbs in parentheses.

● ● ●

Veera is 12. She [1] _goes_ (go) to school in Finland, and her class [2] _____ (have) 18 students. School [3] _____ (start) at 9:45 a.m., and it [4] _____ (end) at 2:45 p.m. There are three or four classes a day. In Finland, students [5] _____ (not have) homework or exams. Veera [6] _____ (have) a lot of free time. After school, she [7] _____ (meet) her friends and they [8] _____ (go) to a sports club for lunch. Veera [9] _____ (love) sports, and she [10] _____ (play) on the school soccer team. Her dream is to be a soccer player!

4 ⭐ Match the adverbs of frequency with the correct meanings.

1 always   [c]   a ✓✓

2 usually   [ ]   b ✗

3 often   [ ]   c ✓✓✓✓

4 sometimes   [ ]   d ✓

5 never   [ ]   e ✓✓✓

5 ⭐ Are these statements true for you? Write *T* (true) or *F* (false).

1 I often do my homework with my friends. ____

2 I always check my phone when I wake up. ____

3 My best friend sometimes has lunch at my house. ____

4 I never go to bed late on the weekend. ____

5 I usually have lunch with my grandparents on Sundays. ____

6 ⭐⭐ Write the words in the correct order to make sentences.

1 makes / dad / often / dinner / My

   My dad often makes dinner.

2 I / brush / after / teeth / always / my / breakfast

   _____

3 go / at / They / lunchtime / usually / home

   _____

4 sometimes / We / class / are / for / late

   _____

5 I / check / in / never / my / class / phone

   _____

6 does / in / the / Dan / park / homework / his / usually

   _____

VOCABULARY AND LISTENING
Free-Time Activities

1 ☆ **Complete the free-time activity phrases.**

1 play an ins t _ r _ u _ m ent
2 go for a b _ _ e r _ _ e
3 read a book or a ma _ _ _ _ _ _ e
4 chat on _ _ _ _ e
5 play v _ _ _ _ o g _ _ _ _ s
6 make v _ _ _ _ _ s
7 take ph _ _ _ _ s
8 download s _ _ _ _ s
9 listen to m _ _ _ c
10 go sh _ _ _ _ _ _ g
11 hang out with fr _ _ _ _ _ s
12 watch _ V

2 ☆☆ **Complete the sentences with the correct form of phrases from Exercise 1.**

1 Laura often ____downloads songs____ from the Internet – she doesn't buy CDs.
2 When I _____ with my friends, we talk for hours on our computers or phones.
3 I usually meet and _____ in the park after school.
4 Luke's sister plays the guitar, but he doesn't _____ .
5 I use my phone to _____ – my friends are the actors. I sometimes put them on YouTube!
6 They never _____ now. They always find movies and series online.

Street Interviews

🎧 **3** ☆ **Listen to the interviews.** (Circle) the correct answer.
2.01

The interviews are about different …
a school activities.
b free-time activities.
c instruments.

🎧 **4** ☆☆ **Listen again and number the activities in the photos in the order you hear them (1–3).**
2.01

🎧 **5** ☆☆ **Listen again and write A (Alyssa), C (Caleb), or D (Destiny).**
2.01

1 __A__ does his/her activity every day.
2 ____ and ____ do their activities on the weekend.
3 ____ does his/her activity early in the morning.
4 ____ does his/her activity with animals.
5 ____ uses the Internet for his/her activity.
6 ____ wants to do his/her activity as a job.

6 ☆☆☆ **Write about one of your free-time activities. Use the questions below to help you.**

Where? How often? When? Who with?

_____

_____

_____

_____

_____

GRAMMAR IN ACTION
Simple Present: Questions

1 ⭐ **Complete the questions with *Do* or *Does*. Then match them with answers a–f.**

1 ___Do___ you see your friends on the weekend? [b]
2 _____ your parents like the same music? ☐
3 _____ your sister watch TV a lot? ☐
4 _____ your cousin hang out with you? ☐
5 _____ all your family members play an instrument? ☐
6 _____ this schedule have ten subjects? ☐

a No, they don't.
b ~~Yes, I do.~~
c Yes, he does.
d Yes, we do.
e No, she doesn't.
f Yes, it does.

2 ⭐⭐ **Write the words in the correct order to make questions. Use the photos to help you.**

① ② ③
④ ⑤ ⑥

1 friends / you / online / Do / your / chat / with / ?
_Do you chat online with your friends?_____

2 download / your / Does / best friend / songs / ?
_____

3 go / for / Do / you / Sundays / a / bike / ride / on / ?
_____

4 shopping / Do / you / go / a lot / ?
_____

5 play / games / your / dad / video / Does / ?
_____

6 your / books / Does / read / aunt / ?
_____

3 ⭐⭐ **Answer the questions in Exercise 2 for you. Use short answers.**

1 _____ 4 _____
2 _____ 5 _____
3 _____ 6 _____

Wh- Questions

4 ⭐ **Circle the correct question words.**

1 (What) / When do you do on the weekend?
2 Where / Who do you go after school?
3 What / Who does Eric have lunch with?
4 Where / What do you usually meet Ava?
5 How often / Who do they go shopping?
6 Where / What time do you wake up on Mondays?

5 ⭐⭐ **Read the interview with a tennis player. Complete the questions using the words in parentheses.**

JADE	What time ¹ _do you get up_ (you / get up), Alina?
ALINA	Very early! At six o'clock.
JADE	² _____ (you / get up) early on weekends, too?
ALINA	No, not always.
JADE	And how often ³ _____ (you / hang out) with friends?
ALINA	I see my friends twice a week.
JADE	⁴ _____ (your friends / come) to your matches?
ALINA	Yes, sometimes they do.
JADE	Great! And ⁵ _____ (your parents / watch) you, too?
ALINA	Yes. My dad comes to all my matches.
JADE	Nice! And ⁶ _____ (other people / ask) you to do interviews?
ALINA	No, they don't! I'm not famous!

WRITING

An Article

1 ⭐ **Read the article. (Circle) the correct title.**

a What does Zev do on the weekend?

b What is Zev's daily routine?

Zev is an American student. He's 12 years old. In his free time, he's a photographer. Zev's photos are of animals and objects. He often makes photo stories. He uses digital technology and his imagination.

1 This is a typical day in Zev's life. He always gets up at 7:00 and takes a shower. At 7:30, he has breakfast. At 7:45, he brushes his teeth and packs his bag. He then goes to school at 8:00.

2 In the afternoon, Zev goes home. At 3:00, he usually has lunch and does his homework. He goes for a walk with his sister at 5:00 and looks for ideas for his photo stories.

3 From 6:30 to 8:00 in the evening, Zev makes his photo stories and puts them on his website. He sometimes chats online with his friends, but he never stays up late. At 9:30, Zev goes to bed.

One day, I want to take photos like Zev!

2 **Match topics a–c with paragraphs 1–3.**

a description of Zev's evening routine ☐

b description of his morning routine ☐

c description of his afternoon routine ☐

3 ⭐ **Read the article again. What time does Zev do these things?**

1 gets up _____7:00_____

2 has breakfast _____

3 packs his bag _____

4 goes to school _____

5 has lunch _____

6 goes for a walk _____

7 makes his photo stories _____

8 goes to bed _____

4 ⭐ **Find and <u>underline</u> five adverbs of frequency in the article.**

5 ⭐⭐ **Rewrite the sentences with the correct punctuation.**

1 how does Zev make his photo stories

How does Zev make his photo stories?

2 zevs sister doesnt take photos

_____

3 zevs friends look at his photo stories

_____

4 wow I think the photos are great

_____

PLAN

6 ⭐⭐ **Write an article about someone's day. Choose a person with a different daily routine than yours. It can be a friend or someone from your family. Decide what information to include in each paragraph. Use the information in Exercise 2 to help you.**

WRITE

7 ⭐⭐⭐ **Write your article. Remember to include the information in the correct order, the simple present, adverbs of frequency, and correct punctuation from the *Useful Language* box (see Student's Book, p29).**

CHECK

8 **Do you …**

• include an interesting title with a question?

• introduce the person, their nationality, and what they do?

• describe the person's morning, afternoon, and evening routines?

• end the article with a sentence about you and your ambition?

VOCABULARY

1 Complete the text with the words in the box.

> brush   do   dressed   get   go (x2)
> have   pack   shower   up

I wake ¹_____ at 6:30, and I
²_____ up at 7:00. Then I take a
³_____ and ⁴_____ my teeth.
I get ⁵_____ and ⁶_____ my bag for
school. At 7:30, I ⁷_____ breakfast with
my mom and dad. I ⁸_____ to school
at 8:30 and finish at 3:30. In the afternoon,
I ⁹_____ my homework, and then I have
some free time. In the evening, I have dinner
with my parents, and then I ¹⁰_____ to
bed at about 10:00.

2 Match the verbs with the activities.

1	chat	☐	a	songs
2	download	☐	b	a bike ride
3	go for	☐	c	online
4	listen to	☐	d	a book or a magazine
5	hang out with	☐	e	music
6	read	☐	f	friends
7	go	☐	g	TV
8	watch	☐	h	shopping

GRAMMAR IN ACTION

3 Complete the sentences with the simple present form of the verbs in parentheses.

1 I _____ (not wake up) early on the weekend.

2 Martin _____ (go) to school at 9:00 every day.

3 We _____ (not do) our homework at school.

4 Tom's dad _____ (make) videos of his birthday every year.

5 Isabela _____ (not have) a big breakfast, only fruit.

6 Theo _____ (not play) the guitar very often.

4 Complete the sentences with the missing words. (Circle) the correct options.

1 Daniel _____ shopping with his mom.
  a sometimes goes   b goes sometimes

2 I _____ video games with my brother.
  a play often   b often play

3 My dad _____ to rock music!
  a listens never   b never listens

4 We _____ with friends on the weekend.
  a always hang out   b hang out always

5 They finish their homework, and they _____ TV.
  a watch often   b often watch

5 Complete the questions and answers with the simple present form of the verbs in parentheses. Add *Wh-* question words where necessary.

1 **A:** _____ you _____ (brush) your teeth every day?   **B:** Yes, I _____.

2 **A:** _____ your mom _____ (pack) your bag for you?   **B:** No, she _____.

3 **A:** _____ your cousins _____ (play) an instrument?   **B:** No, they _____.

4 **A:** _____ time _____ Chris _____ (go) home?   **B:** At 7:00.

5 **A:** _____ often _____ you _____ (read) a book?   **B:** Every month.

6 **A:** _____ you _____ (go) on Sundays?   **B:** I often go to the park with my family.

CUMULATIVE GRAMMAR

6 Complete the conversation with the missing words. (Circle) the correct options.

ROSA	[1] _____ do you do in your free time?
MIRA	I [2] _____ my best friend or go with my brother for a bike ride.
ROSA	[3] _____ you see your best friend every day?
MIRA	Yes, most days. [4] _____ 's your best friend?
ROSA	That's Susan, but I [5] _____ her all the time.
MIRA	[6] _____ often do you see her?
ROSA	It depends, but usually every weekend. We sometimes [7] _____ basketball on Saturdays.
MIRA	Hey! I play, too. What [8] _____ do you meet on Saturdays?
ROSA	Usually in the afternoon.
MIRA	[9] _____ to hang out one Saturday?
ROSA	Sure! [10] _____ your phone? Here's my number.
MIRA	Yes, I [11] _____ . OK, great!

1 a What   b Where
2 a meet usually   b usually meet
3 a Does   b Do
4 a Who   b When
5 a don't see   b doesn't see
6 a When   b How
7 a play   b plays
8 a often   b time
9 a You want   b Do you want
10 a Have do you   b Do you have
11 a do   b do have

3 How do we learn?

VOCABULARY
School Subjects

1 ⭐ Complete the subjects with the correct letters.

1 Eng⌐ish
2 Spani__h
3 vocatio__al educati__n
4 m__th
5 musi__
6 ar__
7 d__ama
8 geo__raphy
9 histor__
10 nut__ition
11 P__
12 sci__nce
13 I__

2 ⭐ Write the correct school subjects from Exercise 1.

1 ____music____

2 _____

3 _____

4 _____

5 _____

6 _____

7 _____

8 _____

3 ⭐⭐ Write the subjects for the definitions.

1 You learn to play an instrument. ____music____
2 You learn a language that people speak in a lot of countries in South America. _____
3 You learn about people, countries, and places. _____
4 You learn about things in the past. _____
5 You learn about numbers, shapes, and space. _____
6 You learn a language that people speak in the UK and the United States. _____
7 You learn about food and what is good or bad to eat. _____
8 You do experiments. _____

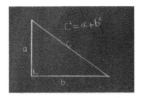 

4 ⭐⭐ Write the names of these subjects in your language. Write *S* if they are similar to the words in English, or *D* if they are different.

1 science _____ __
2 geography _____ __
3 drama _____ __
4 art _____ __

Explore It! 🖱

Guess the correct answer.
One school in Lucknow, India, has a lot of students. How many students does it have?
a about 15,000   b about 27,000   c about 52,000

Find another interesting fact about school subjects in another country. Write a question and send it to a classmate in an email, or ask them in the next class.

READING

A Webpage

1 ⭐ Read the webpage about schools in Singapore. Why don't teachers like posters in math classrooms?

_____

● ● ●

SCHOOLS IN SINGAPORE

HOME | STORIES | PHOTOS

STUDENTS FROM SINGAPORE OFTEN GET VERY GOOD SCORES IN MATH AND SCIENCE ON INTERNATIONAL TESTS.

In math classes, students can use technology to answer the different math problems. Their answers go on the whiteboard at the front of the class. All students can see and talk about their classmates' answers.

A lot of math classrooms don't have posters on the walls. Teachers don't think posters help students learn.

Students can't talk to each other a lot. They work alone, but they can ask the teacher questions when they don't understand something.

In science classes, students can work on their projects once a week. In one class, they can build a robotic arm, and in another class, students can make a small radio.

In many high schools in Singapore, students don't do a lot of drama, language, music, or art. Some teachers say, "Art subjects aren't very important. Students need to be good at science and math. They need these subjects for their adult life."

Is this a good or a bad idea? What do you think?

2 ⭐⭐ Read the webpage again and <u>underline</u> these words. Then check their meaning in a dictionary and complete the sentences.

> ~~adult~~   alone   build
> scores   whiteboard

1 In many countries, you're an
   ____adult____ when you're 18.

2 My teacher always writes the answers on the _____.

3 I never get good _____ on geography tests. Maps are difficult!

4 We want to _____ a robot for our project.

5 **A:** Do you need help?
   B: No, thanks. I always do my homework _____.

3 ⭐⭐ Answer the questions.

1 What subjects are students from Singapore often good at?
   _____math and science_____

2 What do teachers show on the whiteboard?
   _____

3 How do students work in math classes?
   _____

4 How often do students work on science projects?
   _____

5 Which subjects are not very important in many schools?
   _____

4 ⭐⭐⭐ Answer the questions with your own ideas.

1 "Art subjects aren't very important." What do you think?
   _____

2 Which subjects do you think are important? Why?
   _____

GRAMMAR IN ACTION
Can for Ability and Permission

1 ⭐ (Circle) **the options that are true for you.**

1 In our classes, we *can / can't* put posters on the walls.

2 At break time, we *can / can't* play and talk to friends.

3 We *can / can't* talk in science classes.

4 We *can / can't* build interesting things for our projects.

5 Sometimes we *can / can't* work in groups in our English classes.

2 ⭐⭐ **Complete the sentences. Use *can/can't* and the verbs in parentheses.**

1 My dad ___can't sing___ because he doesn't have a good voice, but he _____ amazing pictures. (sing / draw)

2 My cousin _____ good photos, but she _____ videos. She's really bad at it! (take / make)

3 My mom _____ salsa very well, and she _____ the guitar, too. She's really good at it! (dance / play)

4 My little brother's four. He _____ English very well, but he _____ it. (speak / read)

3 ⭐⭐ **Complete the texts with *can/can't* and the verbs in parentheses.**

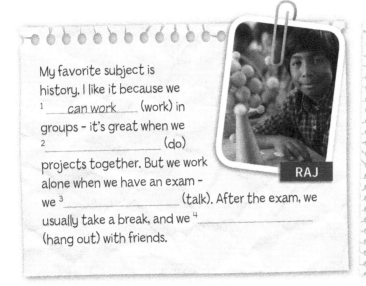

My favorite subject is history. I like it because we
1 ___can work___ (work) in groups - it's great when we
2 _____ (do) projects together. But we work alone when we have an exam - we 3 _____ (talk). After the exam, we usually take a break, and we 4 _____ (hang out) with friends.

RAJ

4 ⭐⭐ **Write questions and short answers with *can.***

1 students / check their phone / in class? (✗)
   Can students check their phone in class?
   No, they can't.

2 students / ask questions / in class? (✓)
   _____
   _____

3 Kate / play the piano? (✓)
   _____
   _____

4 María / speak two languages? (✗)
   _____
   _____

5 students / work in groups / in math classes? (✓)
   _____
   _____

6 he / do ballet? (✗)
   _____
   _____

5 ⭐⭐ **Are these statements true for you? Write *T* (true) or *F* (false).**

1 I can speak two languages. ____

2 I can dance salsa. ____

3 I can ride a bike. ____

4 I can play the guitar. ____

5 I can sing. ____

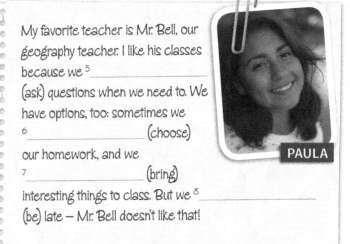

My favorite teacher is Mr. Bell, our geography teacher. I like his classes because we 5 _____ (ask) questions when we need to. We have options, too: sometimes we 6 _____ (choose) our homework, and we 7 _____ (bring) interesting things to class. But we 8 _____ (be) late – Mr. Bell doesn't like that!

PAULA

VOCABULARY AND LISTENING

Places in a School

1 ⭐ Read the definitions. Then (circle) the correct places in the spidergram.

1 You can do outdoor sports here.
2 You can buy and eat food here.
3 You can do PE here.
4 Teachers can plan their lessons here.
5 You can leave your bag here.
6 You can read books and study here.
7 You can wash your hands here.

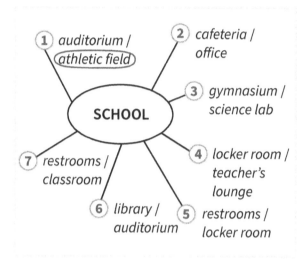

1 auditorium / (athletic field)
2 cafeteria / office
3 gymnasium / science lab
4 locker room / teacher's lounge
5 restrooms / locker room
6 library / auditorium
7 restrooms / classroom

SCHOOL

2 ⭐⭐ Complete the text with places from Exercise 1.

A Radio Program

🎧 **3** 3.01 ⭐⭐ Listen and number the places in the order you hear them (1–6).

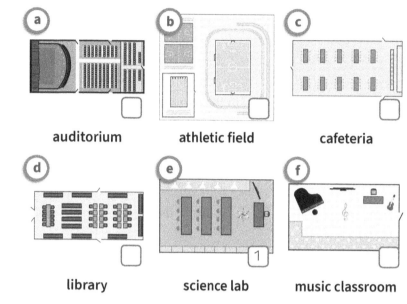

a auditorium
b athletic field
c cafeteria
d library
e science lab [1]
f music classroom

🎧 **4** 3.01 ⭐⭐ Listen again. Are the sentences *T* (true) or *F* (false)?

1 Alex likes the science lab. T
2 He likes the magazines from the library. ___
3 Alex's favorite subject is PE. ___
4 The music classroom is Alex's favorite place. ___
5 Marina has lunch in the cafeteria. ___
6 She likes all the places in the school. ___

Mondays!

I don't like my schedule on Mondays! At 8:45, I go to the ¹ _____office_____ and say hello to my aunt – she works at the school. Then I go to the ² _____ and put my sports shoes in my locker. After that, my class goes to the ³ _____ and we do experiments. I don't like science! At break time, I usually go to the ⁴ _____ for some food. Then we have PE in the ⁵ _____ and then lunch. In the afternoon, it's music and drama. At 4:15, we go to the ⁶ _____ and get a book to read – that's OK because I like books, but I'm always happy on Mondays at 4:30 because I can go home!

GRAMMAR IN ACTION

Verb Forms: (Don't) Like, Don't Mind, Love, Hate + -ing

1 ⭐ **Match the verbs with the emojis.**

1 love [b] 2 like [ ] 3 don't mind [ ]
4 don't like [ ] 5 hate [ ]

a 😕 b 😍 c 😠 d 😀 e 😐

2 ⭐⭐ **Write sentences with the correct form of the verbs.**

1 I / like / go / to the music club
 I like going to the music club.

2 We / hate / have / a lot of homework
 _____

3 Tariq / not mind / play / sports in the gymnasium
 _____

4 Gina / love / play / soccer / on the athletic field
 _____

5 They / not like / learn / history
 _____

3 ⭐⭐ **Complete the text with the correct form of the verbs in parentheses.**

> I have a twin brother, but we're very different!
> He ¹ *hates getting up* (hate / get up) early, but I ² _____ (not mind / do) it for school. He ³ _____ (love / play) sports, and I ⁴ _____ (like / play) video games. I ⁵ _____ (not like / go) to parties. I ⁶ _____ (like / stay) at home. My brother ⁷ _____ (love / hang out) with his friends and ⁸ _____ (have) a good time. He ⁹ _____ (not mind / study) sometimes, but he doesn't love it. I ¹⁰ _____ (love / learn) new things, especially about science.

Object Pronouns

4 ⭐ **Complete the chart with the object pronouns.**

Subject	I	you	he	she	it	we	they
Object	¹ me	²	³	⁴	⁵	⁶	⁷

5 ⭐ (Circle) **the correct option.**

1 **A:** Do you like drama? **B:** Yes, I like (it) / them.
2 Mr. Patel isn't in the office. Can you call her / him?
3 I have a problem. Can you help me / it, please?
4 Is Amaya here? I can't see you / her.
5 **A:** Do you like video games? **B:** I hate it / them.
6 What classes do we have today? Can you give us / you the schedule, please?

6 ⭐⭐ **Look at the pictures and then complete the text with the correct subject or object pronouns.**

Me (Josh)   Lucas

Lucas' mom   Spanish   ¡HOLA!

I'm Josh, and Lucas is my best friend.
¹ _We_ (👦 + 👦) 're in the same class and ² _____ (👦) lives near ³ _____ (👦). Lucas' mom is Spanish. ⁴ _____ (👩) speaks Spanish with ⁵ _____ (👦) at home, but ⁶ _____ (👦) speak English with ⁷ _____ (👦 + 👩). We learn Spanish at school, and Lucas helps ⁸ _____ (👦) with my homework. Spanish is difficult, but I like ⁹ _____ (¡HOLA!).

WRITING

A Description

1 ⭐ **Read Sanjiv's description. Does he like his school?**

_____

My School

[1] Tracks and Subjects

I study at a very big school. Students can take different tracks, <u>such as</u> science or arts. I'm on the science track. I study English, math, and science, and technology subjects, <u>like</u> computer science. That's my favorite subject.

[2] _____

I really like the teachers. They teach regular classes, but they also teach some after-school clubs, <u>like</u> astronomy and dance. I like being with my teachers after class.

[3] _____

We have six classes a day and homework. I don't mind doing some homework, but I don't like a lot of it! I really like working with my classmates on group projects. I don't like working alone!

[4] _____

Our school has great places for classes and activities. <u>For example</u>, we have a big gymnasium, a cafeteria, a computer lab, and three science labs. I love studying here.

2 ⭐ **Write the correct heading for each paragraph in the description.**

Great Teachers ~~Tracks and Subjects~~

School Places School Routine

3 ⭐ **Read the description again. Then complete the text below with the phrases in the box.**

> computer science   doing a lot of homework
> ~~the teachers at his school~~   working alone

Sanjiv likes [1] _____the teachers at his school_____ and
[2] _____ . He doesn't like
[3] _____ or
[4] _____ .

4 ⭐ **Look at the <u>underlined</u> words and phrases in Sanjiv's description. What does he use them for? (Circle) the correct answer.**

a to join ideas

b to show different times

c to give examples

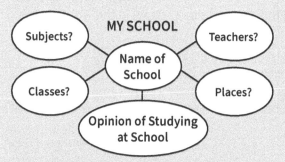

PLAN

5 ⭐⭐ **Write a description of your school. Make a spidergram of your school in your notebook and use the plan below.**

MY SCHOOL

Subjects? — Name of School — Teachers?

Classes? — Places?

Opinion of Studying at School

6 **Decide what information to include in each paragraph. Use your spidergram and the information in Exercise 2 to help you.**

WRITE

7 ⭐⭐⭐ **Write your description. Remember to include four paragraphs, *can/can't*, and expressions from the *Useful Language* box (see Student's Book, p41).**

CHECK

8 **Do you ...**

- give the name of the school in the opening sentence?
- include all of the information from your spidergram?
- give your opinion about studying at the school in your closing sentence?

VOCABULARY

1 **Complete the school subjects.**

1 Languages: E_ _ _ _ _ _ _ , S_ _ _ _ _ _

2 Numbers: m_ _ _

3 The past: h_ _ _ _ _ _

4 Countries: g_ _ _ _ _ _ _ _

5 In a lab: s_ _ _ _ _ _

6 Art subjects: d_ _ _ _ , m_ _ _ _ _ , a_ _

7 Sports: p_ _ _ _ _ _ _   e_ _ _ _ _ _ _

8 IT: i_ _ _ _ _ _ _ _ _   t_ _ _ _ _ _ _ _

9 Food: n_ _ _ _ _ _ _

2 **Find 12 places in a school in the word search.**

O	L	H	W	L	I	B	R	A	R	Y	P	S	O
T	E	A	C	H	E	R	S	L	O	U	N	G	E
C	Y	C	A	F	E	T	E	R	I	A	I	U	T
L	O	C	K	E	R	R	O	O	M	E	G	M	W
A	Z	G	Y	M	N	A	S	I	U	M	F	R	P
S	A	T	H	L	E	T	I	C	F	I	E	L	D
S	P	A	U	D	I	T	O	R	I	U	M	T	W
R	S	C	I	E	N	C	E	L	A	B	A	B	T
O	O	H	O	P	R	E	S	T	R	O	O	M	S
O	C	T	B	G	N	G	T	O	F	F	I	C	E
M	W	B	U	F	T	A	P	F	Y	E	I	D	B
C	O	M	P	U	T	E	R	L	A	B	N	F	T

GRAMMAR IN ACTION

3 **Look at the chart. Complete the sentences with *can/can't* and the correct verbs.**

1 Jon _____ the guitar.

2 Lisa _____ the guitar.

3 _____ Jon _____ songs in English? _____ , he _____ .

4 _____ Lisa _____ songs in English? _____ , she _____ .

5 Jon and Lisa _____ Spanish.

4 Look at the symbols. Write sentences using (*don't*) *like, don't mind, love, hate* + *-ing*.

1 We / 😃 / talk to / our teachers _____

2 I / 😕 / do / homework _____

3 She / 😍 / listen / to music _____

4 They / 😐 / have / lunch at school _____

5 He / 😠 / be / late for class _____

5 Match questions 1–6 with answers a–f.

1 Does Tom like soccer? ☐

2 Does Beth play video games? ☐

3 Can you help Suzi? ☐

4 Is Harry in your class? ☐

5 Is this party for you and your friends? ☐

6 Do you like reading? ☐

a No, it isn't for us!

b No, he hates it!

c I don't mind it.

d Yes, she loves them.

e Yes, I can help her.

f Yes, he is.

CUMULATIVE GRAMMAR

6 Complete the conversation with the missing words. (Circle) the correct options.

DENIZ   Hi, Kate! ¹_____ soccer today?

KATE   No, I ²_____ . It's Wednesday today.

DENIZ   When ³_____ practice?

KATE   On Tuesdays and Thursdays, and on the weekend ⁴_____ have games.

DENIZ   Oh! And ⁵_____ your parents watch your games?

KATE   It depends. ⁶_____ come and see me.

DENIZ   Hey, ⁷_____ do we finish school today?

KATE   At three o'clock! It's Wednesday, remember?

DENIZ   Oh, great! Harry and I ⁸_____ for a bike ride after school on Wednesdays.

KATE   ⁹_____ Harry now?

DENIZ   He's in the library. He ¹⁰_____ a math project to finish.

KATE   Well, I love ¹¹_____ my bike. ¹²_____ I go with you?

DENIZ   Sure!

1	a	Do you have	b	Have you	c	You have
2	a	doesn't	b	don't have	c	don't
3	a	do you have	b	have you	c	you have
4	a	always we	b	we always	c	it always
5	a	does	b	do	c	are
6	a	They sometimes	b	Them sometimes	c	Sometimes them
7	a	when	b	who	c	what
8	a	go usually	b	usually goes	c	usually go
9	a	What's	b	Where's	c	Who's
10	a	has	b	have	c	don't have
11	a	riding	b	ride	c	rides
12	a	Do	b	Can	c	Have

4 What do you like to eat?

VOCABULARY
Food and Drink

1 ⭐ **Complete the chart with the words in the box.**

> ~~apples~~   bananas   cheese   chicken
> eggs   fish   juice   rice   soda

Food from Plants	Food from Animals	Drinks
apples		

2 ⭐⭐ Circle **the correct answers in the quiz.**

ALL ABOUT FOOD AND DRINK

1 Which food is NOT usually a cake?
  a chicken   **b** chocolate

2 Which of these is NOT protein?
  a meat   **b** carrots

3 Which of these is NOT from fruit?
  a juice   **b** chocolate

4 Which of these is NOT from a plant?
  a meat   **b** rice

3 ⭐⭐ **Complete the food words in the text.**

I'm Zara from Malaysia. I usually have kaya toast with ¹e_g_g_s for breakfast. I have lunch at school. Lunch is usually rice and ²me___ or ³ch_____ curry with vegetables. I drink ⁴ju_____ made from oranges and purple ⁵ca_____ and red ⁶ap_____. It's yummy! My mom cooks dinner. I love her ⁷fi___ curry with ⁸be____. We always drink ⁹w_____.

4 ⭐⭐⭐ **What is your favorite food for breakfast, lunch, and dinner? Write about what you eat. Use Exercise 3 to help you.**

I usually have …_____

_____

_____

Explore It! 🖱

Guess the correct answer.
Which country grows millions of bananas?

a the United States   **b** Ecuador
  c China

Find another interesting fact about food in your country. Write a question and send it to a classmate in an email, or ask them in the next class.

READING

An Article

1 ⭐ **Read the article and match the foods in the box with the photos (1–3).**

> blinis   herring with potatoes   mooncakes

Welcome to My Festival!

1 _____

2 _____

3 _____

Hugo:
Midsummer Eve, Sweden

I love this festival in June. It's at the beginning of summer vacation. We go to the country, and in the morning, we get some flowers for our hair. Then we dance to traditional music. Lunch is outside, and it's big! We always eat herring (a type of fish) with potatoes. Later, people play instruments and dance all night!

Mei Lin:
Moon Festival, China

My favorite festival is in September, when we can see the first full moon of the month. We make paper lights and go to the park. And of course, we eat a mooncake or two! These are small round cakes (like the moon!) that have different fillings. I like the chocolate one. We give them to our friends and eat them together.

Daria:
Maslenitsa Pancake Festival, Russia

This great festival is in February. We have fun activities for seven days! We do some sports, play music, dance, and eat a lot of food. I love having blinis. They are Russian pancakes made with butter, eggs, and milk. We eat them with different toppings. My favorite topping is salmon and cream cheese. Yummy!

2 ⭐⭐ **Read the article again and <u>underline</u> these words. Then check their meaning in a dictionary and complete the sentences.**

> country   fillings
> full moon   pancakes   t̶o̶p̶p̶i̶n̶g̶s̶

1 What are your favorite ___toppings___ on a pizza? I love extra cheese!

2 Every four weeks, we can see the _____ in the sky. It's completely round.

3 *Empanadas* are popular in South America. They have different _____ inside, such as meat or vegetables.

4 I love going to the _____ and looking at the trees and flowers.

5 We need milk and butter to make _____ .

3 ⭐⭐ **Read the article again and complete the chart.**

Festival	Country	Month	Special Food
Midsummer Eve	Sweden	1 _June_	2 _____
Moon Festival	3 _____	4 _____	mooncakes
Maslenitsa	5 _____	February	6 _____

4 ⭐⭐⭐ **Answer the questions with your own ideas.**

1 Which of the festivals is your favorite? Why?

_____

2 Think of a festival in your country. When is it? What food do you have?

_____

GRAMMAR IN ACTION
Countable and Uncountable Nouns

1 ⭐ **Write the correct headings in the chart:**
Countable or *Uncountable*.

1 _____	2 _____
cheese water bread _____rice_____ _____ _____	apple egg tomato _____ _____ _____

2 ⭐ **Complete the chart in Exercise 1 with the words in the box.**

> bean   carrot   chocolate   fish   ~~rice~~   taco

A/An, Some/Any

3 ⭐ Ⓒircle **the correct options.**

1 We use *a* or *an* with (countable) / *uncountable* nouns.

2 We use *some* and *any* with *singular* / *plural* countable nouns and uncountable nouns.

3 We use *some* in *affirmative* / *negative* sentences.

4 We use *any* in *affirmative* / *negative* sentences and questions.

4 ⭐⭐ **Complete the sentences with the words in the box.**

> ~~apple~~   chocolate   eggs   juice   sandwich

1 Do you have _____apple_____ for your snack?

2 We don't have any _____ for an omelet.

3 I'm hungry. Do you have a _____ for me?

4 Drink some _____ with your breakfast.

5 Can we have some _____ after dinner?

5 ⭐⭐ **Complete the conversation with *a*, *an*, *some*, or *any*.**

KIM What can we have for dinner? Do we have
¹ _____any_____ rice?

DAN No, we don't have ² _____ rice, but we have ³ _____ pasta.

KIM Pasta with cheese! Do we have ⁴ _____ cheese?

DAN No. I can see ⁵ _____ tomato and ⁶ _____ egg, but that's all! Let's go to the store.

KIM OK. Can you write a list? We need ⁷ _____ cheese, ⁸ _____ milk, and ⁹ _____ tomatoes. Is that all?

DAN No. We don't have ¹⁰ _____ drinks. We need ¹¹ _____ juice.

KIM Right! And ¹² _____ chocolate!

6 ⭐⭐⭐ **What is your favorite dinner? What do you have at home to make it and what do you need? Write sentences with *a*, *an*, *some*, and *any*.**

I want _____ for dinner.

I have _____

I don't have _____

I need _____

VOCABULARY AND LISTENING

Adjectives

1 ☆ Complete the adjectives with the missing vowels. Then match adjectives 1, 5, 7, and 10 with the photos (a–d).

1 h o t [d]
2 d _ l _ c _ _ _ _ s
3 _ nh _ _ lthy
4 d _ sg _ st _ ng
5 sw _ _ t ☐
6 sp _ _ cy
7 c _ ld ☐
8 h _ _ lthy
9 fr _ sh
10 s _ lty ☐

a
b
c
d

2 ☆☆ (Circle) the correct options.

1 Careful! The milk is *cold* / *hot* !
2 I don't like beans. They're *delicious* / *disgusting*!
3 Ice cream is perfect for a hot day. It's *hot* / *cold* and *sweet* / *spicy*.
4 Water is a *healthy* / *unhealthy* drink, but soda is *healthy* / *unhealthy*.
5 I like having *disgusting* / *fresh* fruit for breakfast.

A Quiz

3 🎧 4.01 ☆ Listen to the family. Do they answer all the questions in the quiz?

_____

4 🎧 4.01 ☆ Listen again. Match the foods (1–3) with the restaurants (a–c).

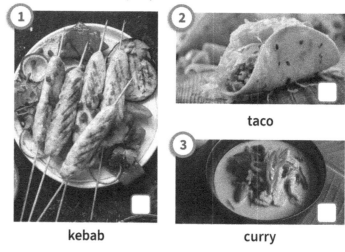

taco

1

kebab

3

curry

a La Cantina   b Kumkapi   c Bangkok Garden

5 🎧 4.01 ☆☆ Listen again. Are the sentences *T* (true) or *F* (false)?

1 The restaurants in the quiz are new. T
2 The names of the restaurants are in the first question.
3 The girl thinks Turkish food is sweet.
4 "Fresh" and "healthy" describe two of the three types of food.
5 The boy thinks kebabs are delicious.
6 The children both want to go to the Mexican restaurant.

6 ☆☆☆ Do you prefer Mexican, Turkish, or Thai food? Look on the Internet for more information about these types of food. Write your ideas.

I prefer _____ food because it's _____

_____

_____

_____

GRAMMAR IN ACTION

There Is/Isn't, There Are/Aren't

1 ⭐ **Look at the picture of the restaurant. Circle the correct options.**

1 There *is* / *isn't* a picture on the wall.

2 There *is some* / *isn't any* water in the glasses.

3 There *is some* / *isn't any* food on the tables.

4 There *are some* / *aren't any* children.

5 There *are* / *aren't* eight people.

6 There *is* / *isn't* a window in the picture.

2 ⭐⭐ **Look at the picture and complete the questions and answers with the correct form of *there is/there are*.**

1 Is there _____ any juice?

    Yes _____ , there is _____ .

2 _____ any bananas?

    _____ , there _____ .

3 _____ any tomatoes?

    _____ , there _____ .

4 _____ any cheese?

    _____ , there _____ .

5 _____ any milk?

    _____ , there _____ .

Much/Many, A Lot Of

3 ⭐⭐ **Circle the correct options.**

My sister loves cooking, and she has [1]*a lot of* / *much* ideas for delicious meals. I like cooking, too, but I don't have [2]*many* / *much* time to help her. She often uses [3]*a lot of* / *much* fruit and vegetables. She loves healthy food. Tonight, she wants to make pasta for dinner, but there isn't [4]*many* / *much* pasta, and there aren't [5]*many* / *much* tomatoes in the fridge. The good thing is that there are [6]*a lot of* / *much* restaurants near home!

4 ⭐⭐ **Complete the questions in the quiz with *much* or *many*. Then circle the correct answers.**

HOW MUCH DO YOU KNOW?

1 How _____ milk is there in 1kg of cheese?

    a two liters   **b** five liters

2 How _____ water is there in a banana?

    a 74%   **b** 90%

3 How _____ sugar is there in an average glass of orange juice?

    a about 21 g   **b** about 50 g

4 How _____ coffee beans are there in a 1-kg bag of coffee?

    a about 1,500   **b** about 8,800

5 ⭐⭐⭐ **Look in your fridge and answer the questions.**

1 How much fruit is there?

_____

2 How many vegetables are there?

_____

WRITING
A Description

1 ⭐ **Look at the menus and read the description. Which menu is from Eva's favorite place, a or b?**

My Favorite Place to Eat
by Eva García

1 My name's Eva ¹(and) / but I'm from Chile. My favorite place to eat is a small café called Buenas Migas. I go there every Friday with my best friend and our parents.

2 Buenas Migas is near my house. There isn't a lot of space inside the café ²and / or it doesn't have many tables, ³or / but there are some more tables outside. We sit outside when the weather's nice.

3 You can eat different sandwiches, and they're all delicious! They have egg, cheese, chicken, ⁴but / or meat sandwiches and they're all healthy. My favorite is the egg sandwich.

4 To drink, you can have water, soda, ⁵but / or juice. Their orange and carrot juice is always fresh. It's definitely my favorite drink!

2 ⭐⭐ ⟨Circle⟩ **the correct options in the description.**

3 ⭐⭐ ⟨Circle⟩ **the correct options.**

We use ¹but / or when there is a choice (usually between two things).
We use ²but / and to contrast different information.
We use ³or / and to add similar information.

4 ⭐⭐ **Read the description again. Match topics a–d with paragraphs 1–4.**

- a food (including your favorite) 3
- b introduction: who you are, what the description is about ...... ☐
- c drinks (including your favorite) ...... ☐
- d the place: where it is and what it is like ...... ☐

a

Menu

Our Sandwiches
egg
meat
cheese
vegetable

Our Cold Drinks
orange juice
water
soda

b

MENU

Our Cold Drinks
orange and carrot juice
water
soda

Our Sandwiches
meat
cheese
egg
chicken

PLAN

5 ⭐⭐ **Write a description of your favorite place to eat. Make notes about the place. Say where it is, when you go there, and what it is like. Decide what information to include in each paragraph. Use the information in Exercise 4 to help you.**

WRITE

6 ⭐⭐⭐ **Write your description. Remember to include four paragraphs, *there is* / *there are*, countable and uncountable nouns, and expressions from the *Useful Language* box (see Student's Book, p53).**

CHECK

7 Do you ...
- introduce yourself and say where you are from and the name of your favorite place?
- say what your favorite type of food and drink is?
- use adjectives to describe food?

VOCABULARY

1 Write the food or drink words. Use the picture to help you.

1 They are a vegetable. They are long and orange.
_ _ _ _ _ _ _

2 You can make cheese from this drink. _ _ _ _ _ _

3 It's usually brown and it's sweet. It's made from cacao. _ _ _ _ _ _ _ _ _

4 It's usually on top of pizza. _ _ _ _ _ _ _

5 They come from chickens. _ _ _ _ _

6 It's a yellow fruit. There are a lot in Ecuador.
_ _ _ _ _ _ _

7 You make this drink with fruit or vegetables.
_ _ _ _ _ _ _

8 It's a drink, but we also use it to take a shower.
_ _ _ _ _

2 Match the opposites.

1	healthy	☐	a disgusting
2	delicious	☐	b sweet
3	cold	☐	c unhealthy
4	salty	☐	d hot

GRAMMAR IN ACTION

3 Circle the correct option: *C* (countable) or *U* (uncountable).

1 apple   C / U
2 cheese   C / U
3 water   C / U
4 sandwich   C / U
5 bread   C / U
6 milk   C / U
7 potato   C / U
8 chocolate C / U
9 banana   C / U
10 bean   C / U

4 Complete the text with *a*, *some*, or *any*.

It's my mom's birthday today, and my dad and I want to make her a nice meal. We don't have ¹_____ chicken, but we have ²_____ meat to cook with ³_____ rice. There's ⁴_____ bottle of water in the fridge and we have ⁵_____ fruit juice, too. There are ⁶_____ carrots and ⁷_____ tomatoes as well. We have ⁸_____ book for my mom. She loves reading.

5 Complete the conversation with the words and phrases in the box.

> Are there any   How many   Is there
> much   some   there are   There aren't

NATHAN Let's make dinner.

ANDREA OK. We can cook some chicken with vegetables. ¹_____ vegetables?

NATHAN Yes, ²_____. We have three carrots and some tomatoes.

ANDREA ³_____ tomatoes are there? I need three.

NATHAN ⁴_____ three – only two.

ANDREA OK. ⁵_____ any cheese? We can have the tomatoes with some cheese.

NATHAN Yes, there's ⁶_____ cheese!

ANDREA Great. And how ⁷_____ chicken is there?

NATHAN A lot! We can eat chicken for dinner, breakfast, and lunch!

CUMULATIVE GRAMMAR

6 Complete the conversation with the missing words. (Circle) the correct options.

VICTOR Mom, what ¹_____ for dinner?

MOM There's ²_____ soup and fish. Do you want that?

VICTOR Yes, I'm hungry! And ³_____ can I have to drink?

MOM ⁴_____ some soda.

VICTOR Do we have any juice? I don't like ⁵_____ soda.

MOM Take a look in the fridge. I think there ⁶_____ two bottles of juice there.

VICTOR Yes! And it's orange juice – delicious! Do you want some juice, too?

MOM No, thanks. I ⁷_____ like it very much. I prefer water. ⁸_____ any apples for after your dinner?

VICTOR No, there ⁹_____ any, but there are some bananas. I ¹⁰_____ eat those.

MOM You're hungry! There's ¹¹_____ food, and you can eat all of it!

VICTOR OK, Mom. Yes, I'm really hungry!

1	a there is	b is there	c are there
2	a some	b a	c an
3	a where	b what	c when
4	a There are	b There is	c There has
5	a drink	b drinking	c drinks
6	a are	b have	c is
7	a do	b don't	c 'm not
8	a Are there	b Is there	c Are they
9	a aren't	b isn't	c haven't
10	a am	b do	c can
11	a much	b a lot of	c many

5 What's your style?

VOCABULARY
Clothes

1 ⭐ Look at the photos and (circle) the correct words.

1 *boots /* (*sneakers*)

2 *hoodie / T-shirt*

3 *jeans / sweatpants*

4 *boots / flip-flops*

5 *shorts / skirt*

6 *T-shirt / jacket*

2 ⭐ Look at the picture. Complete the text with the words in the box.

> boots   cap   jacket   shirt
> shorts   sneakers   sweatpants   ~~T-shirt~~

Laura   Alex

Laura's favorite outfit is a ¹ _____T-shirt_____ ,
² _____ , ³ _____ , and a
⁴ _____ . Alex's favorite outfit is a
⁵ _____ and a ⁶ _____ ,
⁷ _____ , and ⁸ _____ .

3 ⭐⭐⭐ What can you wear? Write at least three clothes items for each situation.

1 Your friends ask you to go to the mountains with them in December.

I can wear _____

2 It's July and you have a picnic with your parents.

_____

3 It's Saturday afternoon and you want to visit your grandma.

_____

Explore It! 🖱

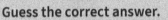 

Guess the correct answer.

A *kurta* is a long shirt without a collar. Men and women from *South America / South Asia / Europe* wear kurtas.

kurta

Find another interesting fact about clothes in your country. Write a question and send it to a classmate in an email, or ask them in the next class.

READING
An Online Diary

1 ⭐ **Read Marina's online diary. Who doesn't like purple?**

_____

Marina'sFashionFriends.com

Sunday, 10:30 a.m.

It's Sunday morning and I'm writing this post from the park. I'm here with my family. I can see a group of girls. They're talking and having some snacks. One girl looks great! I want her clothes! 😃
She's wearing purple jeans, an orange T-shirt, a black cap, and some fabulous purple sneakers. 👍👟 I think those sneakers are in a store around the corner! Hmm … do I have got the money to buy them?

2:00 p.m. (and back online!)

I'm at home and guess what? I have those beautiful sneakers!

6:00 p.m.

Comments

Ethan: Hi, Marina! I always read your diary, and I usually like your ideas. 😌 But sorry … I don't like purple. I think it's a horrible color! 😠 It's a nice day today and I'm at a park, too. I'm wearing my new sweatpants, and a T-shirt, but it's hot now, and I'm not wearing my cap. What are you wearing?

Ada: Where can I buy those sneakers? I want some, too. Ethan, purple is THE color! I have six purple T-shirts and a pair of purple shorts! I'm wearing my favorite purple T-shirt today!

8:00 p.m.

Ada, they're selling them in World of Sneakers. I'm wearing them now! 👖
Now I need some jeans.
Sorry, Ethan, purple is THE color! 😉

New post tomorrow!

2 🌟🌟 **Read the diary again and <u>underline</u> these words. Check their meaning in a dictionary and then complete the sentences.**

> beautiful   corner   ~~fabulous~~
> guess what   pair

1 I love my green boots. They're
   _____fabulous_____ !
2 _____ ? We're in the same class!
3 The store isn't far away. It's around the _____ .
4 Sara's new skirt is _____ . I want one!
5 You need to get a new _____ of shoes.

3 🌟🌟 **Read the diary again. Circle the correct answers.**

1 It's Sunday and Marina _is /_ (_isn't_) at home.
2 She likes _one girl's / some girls'_ sneakers.
3 Ethan _usually likes / doesn't usually like_ Marina's posts.
4 Marina and _Ethan / Ada_ want to buy the sneakers.
5 Ada _has some / doesn't have any_ purple clothes.
6 Marina tells _Ethan / Ada_ the name of a sneakers store.

4 🌟🌟🌟 **Answer the questions with your own ideas.**

1 Do you think fashion is important? Why / Why not?

_____

_____

2 Where do you get your ideas about what to wear? For example, from online diaries, friends, magazines, TV, movies, stores?

_____

_____

GRAMMAR IN ACTION
Present Continuous

1 ⭐⭐ **Write the words in the correct order to make sentences.**

1 on TV / I'm / fashion show / a / watching

I'm watching a fashion show on TV.

2 her / She / isn't / doing / homework

_____

3 the park / sitting / Marina / is / in

_____

4 a / Ethan / isn't / cap / wearing

_____

5 playing / We're / basketball

_____

6 same / skirt / the / buying / They're

_____

2 ⭐⭐ **Complete the message with the correct form of the verb *to be*.**

> 📶   60% 🔋
>
> < Back   ☰
>
> Hi Dad! I ¹___'m___ sitting on the school
> bus and it ²_____ (not) moving!
> The bus driver ³_____ talking on
> the phone, and he ⁴_____ (not)
> looking very happy. Oh, and it
> ⁵_____ raining! Can you come?
> Juan ⁶_____ playing hockey, and
> Mom ⁷_____ (not) answering
> the phone.
> Thanks, Dad!

3 ⭐⭐ **What are they doing? Look at pictures 1–4 and write sentences using the words in boxes a and b.**

a) dance ~~read~~ ride write

b) a bike ~~a magazine~~ on the board to music

1 *He's reading a magazine.*

2 _____

3 _____

4 _____

4 ⭐⭐ **Match questions 1–6 with answers a–f.**

1 Are you listening to me? [b]

2 Is Anton wearing his new sneakers? ☐

3 Is Claudia studying? ☐

4 What are they eating? ☐

5 Which movie is Pedro watching? ☐

6 Where are you having your lunch? ☐

a *Wonder Woman*.

b ~~Yes, I am~~!

c In the cafeteria.

d No, she isn't.

e Cold pizza. Yuck!

f Yes, he is.

5 ⭐⭐⭐ **Answer the questions.**

1 What are you wearing today?

_____

2 What is your best friend doing now?

_____

6 ⭐⭐⭐ **Find out what two people in your family are doing now. Write sentences in the present continuous.**

My sister's watching TV.

_____

_____

_____

VOCABULARY AND LISTENING

Accessories

1 ⭐ **Complete the accessory words in the spidergram.**

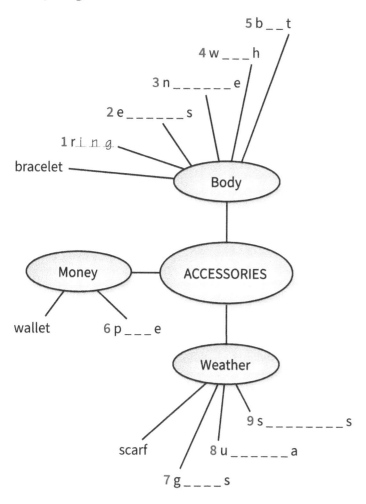

5 b _ _ t
4 w _ _ _ h
3 n _ _ _ _ _ _ e
2 e _ _ _ _ _ _ s
1 r i n g
bracelet

Body

Money
wallet
6 p _ _ _ e

ACCESSORIES

Weather
scarf
8 u _ _ _ _ _ _ a
9 s _ _ _ _ _ _ _ _ s
7 g _ _ _ _ s

2 ⭐⭐ **Complete the sentences with words from Exercise 1.**

1 Those new jeans look big. You need a
___belt___ .

2 José always wears _____ when it's sunny.

3 Madison carries her wallet and phone in her
_____ .

4 I don't wear a _____ because there's a clock in the classroom.

5 It's raining, and I don't have my _____ !

6 In cold weather, my grandma always wears
_____ and a _____ .

7 My dad has a big _____ , but he never has any money in it!

An Interview

🎧 3 ⭐ **Listen to the interview. Mark (✓) the two things that Alba paints.**
5.01

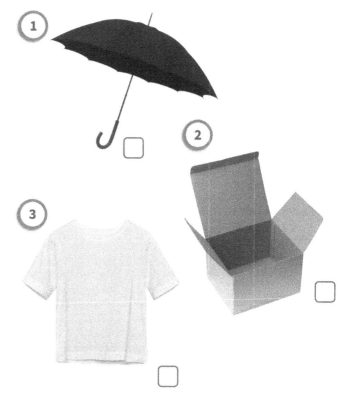

1 ☐

2 ☐

3 ☐

🎧 4 ⭐⭐⭐ **Listen again. Answer the questions.**
5.01

1 Who is Alba painting this week?
Her baby brother.

2 Where does she get her ideas from?
_____

3 What does she put in the mini boxes?
_____

4 What is inside the box for her friend?
_____

5 What does the interviewer want?
_____

5 ⭐ **Alba is making you a box (big or small). Write two things you want to put in it. Use the ideas below or your own ideas.**

> a bracelet   a ring   a wallet   a watch   gloves

I'd like _____ and _____ .

GRAMMAR IN ACTION
Simple Present and Present Continuous

1 ⭐ (Circle) the correct options.

2 We use the *simple present / present continuous* to talk about things happening now.

3 We use the *simple present / present continuous* to talk about facts, habits, and routines.

2 ⭐ Complete the chart with the words and phrases in the box.

> at the moment   every Monday   never
> ~~on Fridays~~   right now   sometimes
> this week   this morning   today   usually

Facts, Habits, and Routines	Things Happening Now
on Fridays	

3 ⭐⭐ Write sentences with the simple present or present continuous.

1 Some people / wear / sports clothes / on the weekend

   Some people wear sports clothes on the weekend.

2 I / look for / some jeans / right now

3 They / make / the costumes for the show / now

4 Naomi / usually / buy / red clothes

5 We / never / go shopping / on Saturdays

6 A lot of people / wear / hats / at the moment

4 ⭐⭐ Complete the conversation with the simple present or present continuous form of the verbs in parentheses.

DANA What ¹ *are you doing* (do), Paula?

PAULA I ² _____ (look) at my clothes. Some of them are very small now. I ³ _____ (often / need) new clothes in the summer.

DANA Oh! Can I have this skirt?

PAULA Well, I ⁴ _____ (always / give) my small clothes to my little sister, but she ⁵ _____ (not wear) skirts, so it's yours!

DANA Thanks! Where ⁶ _____ (you / usually / buy) your clothes?

PAULA At a store near home. My mom ⁷ _____ (shop) there right now.

DANA ⁸ _____ (they / sell) accessories, too? I ⁹ _____ (look for) a bracelet at the moment.

PAULA Yes, they do! They ¹⁰ _____ (sell) lovely bracelets. We can go shopping there together next time!

5 ⭐⭐⭐ Answer the questions.

1 What do you do with your old clothes and accessories?

2 What clothes are you wearing a lot at the moment?

3 What do you usually wear in the evening during the week?

WRITING
A Description of a Photo

1 ⭐ **Read the description and look at the photo. Write the names of the people (a–e).**

a _____Damir_____   d _____

b _____   e _____

c _____

A Photo of a Day Out

By Alyssa

1 This is a photo of my friends and me. We're on a school trip to a national park. It's cold but sunny.

2 The boy on the left is Damir. He [1]*looks* / (*'s looking*) down. He often [2]*looks* / *is looking* down because he hates photos! He [3]*wears* / *'s wearing* a black and gray hoodie. Next to Damir is Peter. He's in a pink shirt and a gray sweater. The boys [4]*don't wear* / *aren't wearing* jackets in the photo. Then that's me in the middle, with a jacket and a checked shirt. Carmen's next to me. She [5]*wears* / *'s wearing* her favorite denim jacket and a big scarf. Gina's on the right. She has a gray T-shirt, a green jacket, and a scarf. Gina's the only one in a hat.

3 This is one of my favorite photos. We [6]*laugh* / *'re laughing* because it's a fun day. I like this photo because there are trees in the back and we all look happy. We always [7]*have* / *are having* a great time!

2 ⭐⭐ Circle **the correct form of the verbs (1–7) in the description.**

3 ⭐⭐ **Read the description again. Complete the sentences with the words in the box.**

| Alyssa   boys   girls   Peter   ~~trees~~ |

1 The _____trees_____ are in the back.

2 _____ is in the middle. Carmen and _____ are next to her.

3 The _____ are on the left.

4 The _____ are on the right.

4 ⭐⭐ **Match topics a–c with paragraphs 1–3.**

a why it is a favorite photo ☐

b people in the photo, where they are, and what they're wearing ☐

c who is in the photo and where the photo is ☐

PLAN

5 ⭐⭐ **Write your own description of a photo of a day out. Choose your photo and make notes. Decide what information to include in each paragraph. Use the information in Exercise 4 to help you.**

WRITE

6 ⭐⭐⭐ **Write your description. Remember to include the information in the correct order, the simple present and present continuous, and expressions from the *Useful Language* box (see Student's Book, p65).**

CHECK

7 **Do you …**

• describe the people in the photo, including the clothes and accessories they are wearing?

• describe the people's positions in the photo?

• say why you like the photo?

VOCABULARY

1 (Circle) the word that doesn't fit.

1 sweatpants / T-shirt / jeans
2 sneakers / shorts / boots
3 shorts / boots / skirt
4 jacket / hoodie / cap
5 shirt / skirt / shorts
6 flip-flops / boots / sneakers

2 Complete the crossword. Use the pictures.

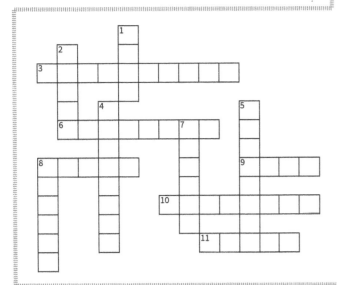

GRAMMAR IN ACTION

3 Complete the sentences with the present continuous form of the verbs in the box.

> do   look   make   not rain
> not wear   watch

1 **A:** What _____ you _____ now?
   B: I'm doing my homework.
2 At the moment, I _____ for a new jacket with my dad.
3 They _____ a TV show about the history of fashion.
4 We _____ our school clothes today – it's Sunday.
5 My grandma _____ me a new dress for my birthday.
6 You don't need an umbrella. It _____ .

ACROSS →

3 6 8
9 10 11

DOWN ↓

1 2 4
5 7 8

4 (Circle) the correct options.

MAYA What ¹*do you usually do / are you usually doing* on the weekend?

ISAAC We ²*sometimes visit / are sometimes visiting* my grandparents, but they ³*travel /'re traveling* around Europe at the moment.

LILY ⁴*Is Jimi having / Does Jimi have* lunch at home this month?

TOM Yes. He usually ⁵*has / is having* lunch at school, but this month he ⁶*goes / 's going* home early.

HUGO ⁷*Does Dad do / Is Dad doing* the shopping now?

CALEB No, it's Sunday. The stores ⁸*close / are closing* early on Sundays.

CUMULATIVE GRAMMAR

5 Complete the conversation with the missing words. (Circle) the correct options.

ADAM Hi, Mom. ¹_____ are you?

MOM Hi, Adam! I'm ²_____ the shopping with Dad.

ADAM Oh, OK! Listen, ³_____ for a bike ride this afternoon with Tom and his brother?

MOM Sure! We don't have ⁴_____ plans.

ADAM Great! But ⁵_____ a problem. I can't ⁶_____ my sneakers, or my hoodie. Where are they?

MOM I ⁷_____ know. They're your things.

ADAM Oh! The sneakers are under my bed, but I can't see my hoodie. Can you buy ⁸_____ a new one, please?

MOM A new one? I don't have ⁹_____ time now, and you have a hoodie! You need to look for ¹⁰_____.

ADAM Ugh! I hate ¹¹_____ things.

MOM I know, but how often ¹²_____ things when you look for them?

ADAM Hmm, I guess so. OK, talk to you later.

1	a When	b Where	c What
2	a does	b do	c doing
3	a can I go	b I can go	c do I go
4	a any	b some	c a
5	a there are	b there's	c it's
6	a find	b to find	c finding
7	a not	b 'm not	c don't
8	a me	b it	c my
9	a many	b any	c a lot
10	a it	b they	c them
11	a look for	b looking for	c looks for
12	a are you finding	b do you find	c you find

6 How can we be athletic?

VOCABULARY
Sports

1 ⭐ **Complete the word puzzle. Use the pictures (1–12). What is the mystery word in gray?**

2 ⭐⭐ **Complete the rules with *play*, *do*, or *go*.**

We usually use ¹_____ with sports that end in *-ing*.

We usually use ²_____ with sports with balls and other objects.

We usually use ³_____ with other sports.

3 ⭐⭐ (Circle) **the correct options.**

I like playing sports. At school, we do ¹*running /* (*track and field*) and I like that. Sometimes on the weekend I go ²*swimming / yoga* with my brother. He does ³*gymnastics / football* at an after-school gym and goes ⁴*running / table tennis* twice a week. I don't really like team sports, but in the summer, I sometimes play ⁵*sailing / volleyball* with my friends on the beach. And I love going ⁶*yoga / rock climbing* with my dad in the mountains.

4 ⭐⭐⭐ **Answer the questions.**

1 What are your favorite sports?

_____

2 Do you play sports at school? Which sports?

_____

Explore It! 🖱

Guess the correct answer.

Which sport comes from Canada?

a hockey   b table tennis   c football

Find another interesting fact about sports in your country. Write a question and send it to a classmate in an email, or ask them in the next class.

READING
Online FAQs

1 ⭐ Read the article. What sport is it about? Mark (✓) the correct photo (1–3).

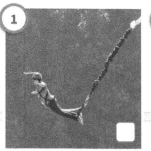

FUN IN THE SUN!

Are you looking for a new sport? Do you want to try something more exciting? In New Zealand, we have the answer – try zorbing! It's new and it's different!

FAQs

Q1: What is Zorbing?

Zorbing is a fun outdoor sport. It's more popular here in New Zealand than in other countries.

Q2: _____

You need a large plastic ball. This is called a zorb. You get inside the ball and run or walk. When you move, the ball moves, too! You know where you're going and how you're moving because you can see through the ball. A lot of people love going down a hill in their zorb. It's exciting!

Q3: _____

No, it's an individual sport. You get inside the zorb on your own, but it's really fun to go with family or friends because you can have races – sometimes children are faster than their parents!

Q4: _____

Yes, it is, but always do it in a zorbing center and follow the rules. Have fun, but be careful – don't get hurt!

Q5: _____

Yes. To go zorbing, you usually need to be six years old or older.

Q6: _____

There are zorbing centers in many places on the South Island. Click here for a list of centers.

Q7: _____

Yes, it's more expensive than other traditional sports, but it's a great activity for special days. So, are you ready for zorbing? What are you waiting for!

2 ⭐⭐ Read the article again. Complete it with the missing questions.
- a Is there an age limit?
- b Is it a team sport?
- c What do you do?
- d ~~What is zorbing?~~
- e Where can I do it?
- f Is it expensive?
- g Is it safe?

3 ⭐⭐ Read the article again and underline these words. Then check their meaning in a dictionary and complete the sentences.

| get hurt   hill   race   ~~safe~~   try |

1 Be careful! Going out alone at night isn't ____safe____ .
2 The Spartathlon is a _____ in Greece. People run 246 kilometers!
3 I live at the top of a _____ . Walking down to school is easy!
4 I love tennis, but this year I want to _____ a new sport.
5 Careful there! You can fall and _____ !

4 ⭐⭐⭐ Answer the questions.

1 Do you want to try zorbing? Why / Why not?

_____
_____
_____
_____

2 What fun outdoor sports are popular in your country?

_____
_____
_____
_____

GRAMMAR IN ACTION
Comparatives

1 ⭐ **Write the comparative forms.**

1 small   4 happy
   smaller   _____

2 big   5 interesting
_____   _____

3 good   6 bad
_____   _____

2 ⭐ **Complete the rules with the adjectives from Exercise 1.**

1 For one-syllable adjectives, add -er:
    smaller   .

2 For two-syllable adjectives ending in -y, remove the -y and add -ier: _____.

3 For long adjectives, add *more* before the adjective: _____.

4 For one-syllable adjectives ending in a vowel and a consonant, double the consonant and add -er: _____.

5 For irregular adjectives, use a different word: _____ and _____.

3 ⭐⭐ <u>Underline</u> **and correct one mistake in each sentence.**

1 Windsurfing is more expensive <u>that</u> running. _____*than*_____

2 Basketball is more fast than football.
_____

3 Runners are usually thiner than swimmers.
_____

4 Which sport is noisyer, volleyball, or yoga?
_____

5 She's badder at gymnastics than at hockey.
_____

6 Playing sports is more better than watching it. _____

4 ⭐⭐ **Complete the sentences with the comparative form of the adjectives in parentheses.**

1 A hockey match is _____*longer*_____ than a basketball game. (long)

2 I think rock climbing is _____ than yoga. (exciting)

3 Lola's _____ at tennis than her dad. (good)

4 Our school hockey team is _____ than the football team. (bad)

5 We think soccer is a _____ game than football. (difficult)

6 Playing sports is _____ than watching TV. (healthy)

5 ⭐⭐ **Complete the questions with a comparative adjective. Then check the answers at the bottom of the page.**

DANIEL Let's do this quiz! First question: Which ball is [1] _____*faster*_____, a table tennis or a tennis ball?

ANIYAH A table tennis ball?

DANIEL Next question: Which is [2] _____, a basketball game or a hockey match?

ANIYAH I don't know. Hockey?

DANIEL Number three: Which country is [3] _____ at table tennis, China or South Korea?

ANIYAH South Korea, I think.

DANIEL And the last question: Which sport is [4] _____ in schools here in New Zealand, hockey or track and field?

ANIYAH Oh, no! I don't know. Track and field maybe. What are the answers?

6 ⭐⭐⭐ **Write three sentences comparing sports. Look at Exercise 4 to help you.**

I think soccer is more entertaining than football. _____

_____

_____

_____

Answers

1 table tennis ball: 116 km/h; tennis ball: 263 km/h

2 hockey match: 60 minutes; basketball game: 48 minutes

3 China (1); South Korea (2)

4 number of people playing in schools in New Zealand: hockey: 13,967, track and field: 12,713

VOCABULARY AND LISTENING
Sports Verbs

1 ⭐ Match photos 1–6 with six of the sports verbs a–l.

> a ~~bounce~~ b catch c climb d dive e hit f jump
> g kick h lift i pass j run k score l throw

1. a
2. ☐
3. ☐
4. ☐
5. ☐
6. ☐

2 ⭐⭐ (Circle) the correct verbs.

I don't understand rugby! OK, the players ¹(pass) / score the ball to each other. Then they ²catch / run up the field and put the ball over a line to ³score / hit points. They also ⁴kick / jump the ball over a big goalpost. But sometimes the teams make a circle and push each other. Then one player ⁵scores / throws the ball into the circle and another player from the same team gets it. And sometimes some players ⁶lift / jump on top of other players!

3 ⭐⭐⭐ Write two sentences describing what players can and can't do in a sport. Use the sports verbs from Exercise 1.

In soccer, the players can kick the ball, but they can't
score goals with their hands.

A Conversation

🎧 6.01 **4** ⭐ Look at the photo and listen to a conversation about goalball, a sport for people who are visually impaired. (Circle) the correct answers.

1 Goalball players use a special ball with *lights / sound*.

2 Goalball is *a team / an individual* sport.

🎧 6.01 **5** ⭐⭐⭐ Listen again. Complete the sentences with one word.

1 The goalball ball is like a __basketball__, but heavier.

2 A goalball team has _____ players on it.

3 Players try to _____ the ball to score a goal.

4 They use their _____ to stop the ball.

5 Some players throw the ball _____ kilometers per hour.

6 Jon plays goalball on a _____ court.

7 The boy wants to watch Jon's match on _____.

6 ⭐⭐⭐ Watch part of a Paralympics goalball match on the Internet. Then write three things you like about it.

I like how the players throw the ball.

GRAMMAR IN ACTION
Superlatives

1 ⭐ Complete the chart with the superlative form of the adjectives in the box.

bad	~~entertaining~~	fit	healthy	old

The most + adjective	*The + double the final consonant + -est*	*The + change y to i + -est*	*The + adjective + -est*	*The + irregular form*
the most popular	2 _____	the easiest	4 _____	the best
1 _the most_ _entertaining_	the biggest	3 _____	the fastest	5 _____

2 ⭐⭐ Complete the text with the superlative form of the adjectives in parentheses.

My cousin Nick is the ¹ _most popular_ (popular) person in my family. He's the ² _____ (tall) of my cousins and also the ³ _____ (fit) – on the weekend, he does yoga and plays hockey! Everybody loves Nick.

He's the ⁴ _____ (happy) person I know! I'm the ⁵ _____ (young) person in my family and the ⁶ _____ (bad) at sports! But that's OK because we're all different. I love reading and writing stories. Nick says I write the ⁷ _____ (interesting) stories in the world.

3 ⭐⭐ Write the questions in the quiz using the superlative form of the adjectives. Then (circle) the correct answers. Check your answers at the bottom of the quiz!

SPORTS QUESTION TIME!

1 Which is / popular / sport in Brazil?
Which is the most popular sport in Brazil?
a basketball   **ⓑ** soccer

2 Which is one of the / old / ball sports?
_____
a Ulama from Mexico
b Alama from Ecuador

3 Which is one of the / new / sports?
_____
a table tennis
b 360Ball

4 Which is one of the / difficult / sports for many people?
_____
a rock climbing **b** running

5 Which is one of the / expensive / sports in the world?
_____
a tennis   **b** swimming

ANSWERS
1b 2a 3b 4a 5a

4 ⭐⭐⭐ Complete the questions with the superlative form of the adjectives. Then answer them for you.

1 Who is _the youngest_ (young) person in your family?
_____

2 Which is _____ (popular) sport at your school?
_____

3 Which is _____ (difficult) school subject?
_____

4 Which is _____ (entertaining) movie you know?
_____

WRITING

A Profile of an Athlete

1 ⭐ **Look at the photos and read the profile. Then complete the sentence.**

For Ivan, Natalia Partyka is an _____ athlete because she plays table tennis with _____ .

A Popular Athlete from My Country

By Ivan Nowak

1 I'm from Poland, and I think one of the ¹*more / most* popular athletes from my country is Natalia Partyka. She's a table tennis player. She's 1.73 m tall and weighs 64 kg. She only has one hand and part of her right arm.

2 Natalia trains for about six hours a day. She often plays with her ²*older / more older* sister, Sandra. Sometimes she practices bouncing the ball on the top part of her arm to begin the game. In her free time, Natalia loves reading the letters from her fans. She also likes going to the beach with her friends.

3 I think Natalia is the ³*more / most* amazing athlete from my country because she plays with one hand. She's also an excellent athlete – she's part of the Paralympic team and the Olympic Games team, too. She has more gold medals than any other table tennis player in Poland, and she's one of the ⁴*most / more* successful players in the world, too.

2 ⭐⭐ (Circle) **the correct options (1–4) in the profile.**

3 ⭐⭐ **Read the profile again.** Underline **two sentences with *also* and two sentences with *too*. Then complete the rules with *also* or *too*.**

We use *too* and *also* to give extra information. We use ¹_____ at the end of a sentence. We use ²_____ after the verb *to be* and before other verbs.

4 ⭐⭐ **Read the profile again. Match topics a–c with paragraphs 1–3.**

a training and other interests ☐
b achievements ☐
c basic information and description ☐

PLAN

5 ⭐⭐ **Write a profile of a popular athlete from your country. Make notes about the athlete. Decide what information to include in each paragraph. Use the information in Exercise 4 to help you.**

WRITE

6 ⭐⭐⭐ **Write your profile. Remember to include three paragraphs, comparatives and superlatives, and expressions from the *Useful Language* box (see Student's Book, p77).**

CHECK

7 Do you …
- give basic information and a description of your athlete?
- describe their sport using sports verbs?
- talk about their achievements and why you like them?

VOCABULARY

1 Complete the chart with the sports in the box.

> football   running   sailing
> swimming   tennis   track and field
> volleyball   windsurfing   yoga

Water Sports	Ball Sports	Other Sports

2 Find 12 sports verbs in the word search.

B	D	I	B	T	D	I	V	E	H
U	I	C	S	D	Q	H	G	R	I
V	O	L	I	F	T	A	H	B	T
Y	K	I	C	K	R	Z	O	S	P
E	C	M	W	Q	M	N	S	C	A
N	P	B	O	U	N	C	E	O	L
L	Y	K	J	C	J	A	T	R	U
T	H	R	O	W	V	T	G	E	R
H	J	U	M	P	W	C	E	F	U
F	P	A	S	S	K	H	X	G	N

3 Complete the sentences with the correct form of the verbs from Exercise 2.

1 A basketball player b_____ the ball on the court.

2 My brother loves j_____ on the bed!

3 Mount Everest, the highest mountain in the world, is very difficult to c_____ .

4 We never s_____ many goals in soccer.

5 Tennis players can't h_____ the ball with their hands. They use a racket.

6 In gymnastics, we sometimes l_____ heavy boxes to make our arms strong.

GRAMMAR IN ACTION

4 Write sentences using the comparative form of the adjectives in parentheses.

1 zorbing / running (exciting)

_____

2 water / soda (healthy)

_____

3 sweatpants / jeans (comfortable)

_____

4 a table tennis ball / a tennis ball (small)

_____

5 jumping / rock climbing (easy)

_____

5 Complete the text with the superlative form of the adjectives in parentheses.

I think tennis is the ¹_____ (boring) sport, but my dad loves it! At the moment, he's in London at the All England Club. This club is the ²_____ (old) in the world. Every year, there are different tennis tournaments there. The ³_____ (popular) one is called Wimbledon. My dad says all the ⁴_____ (good) players want to win there. People watching tennis at Wimbledon don't usually speak to each other a lot. The ⁵_____ (bad) thing you can do at Wimbledon is talk! The players don't like noise. I think the ⁶_____ (easy) thing is to watch Wimbledon on TV, but not for me – I prefer a good movie!

CUMULATIVE GRAMMAR

6 Complete the conversation with the missing words. (Circle) the correct options.

ESMA	Which sports ¹_____ you like, Rafael?
RAFAEL	I like ²_____ track and field and playing baseball.
ESMA	I think baseball is the ³_____ sport in the world.
RAFAEL	Me, too! Today, I ⁴_____ baseball practice and then yoga.
ESMA	Yoga! I think it's ⁵_____ than track and field!
RAFAEL	Then try it with me! I can teach you the ⁶_____ exercises.
ESMA	Sounds great, but I'm the ⁷_____ student in the world!
RAFAEL	Ah! But I'm a ⁸_____ teacher!
ESMA	OK! I ⁹_____ try.
RAFAEL	¹⁰_____ your sweatpants in your bag?
ESMA	No, but I can ¹¹_____ home and get them now.
RAFAEL	Perfect. Run home and bring ¹²_____ sweatpants!

1	a	does	b	are	c	do
2	a	does	b	do	c	doing
3	a	best	b	better	c	good
4	a	has	b	have	c	having
5	a	most interesting	b	more interesting	c	interesting
6	a	more easy	b	most easy	c	easiest
7	a	bad	b	worse	c	worst
8	a	good	b	the better	c	best
9	a	can	b	have	c	do
10	a	Do you have	b	Do have	c	You have
11	a	go to	b	go	c	come
12	a	yours	b	you	c	your

7 Why are animals important?

VOCABULARY
Animals

1 ⭐ **Find 13 more words for animals in the word search.**

C	R	O	C	O	D	I	L	E	D	E	Y
H	I	P	P	O	B	D	O	N	K	E	Y
J	L	S	I	S	W	A	Y	U	K	A	G
P	H	W	B	C	N	G	D	N	T	G	I
A	M	H	E	K	M	A	N	I	J	L	R
R	Q	O	A	V	I	D	K	T	H	E	A
R	K	R	R	P	L	U	Z	E	B	C	F
O	R	S	O	E	N	C	D	W	V	E	F
T	X	E	G	T	W	K	M	O	U	S	E
Z	F	W	H	A	L	E	G	K	S	B	A
A	N	F	M	P	B	M	O	N	K	E	Y
L	I	O	N	V	T	C	N	U	I	J	X

2 ⭐ (Circle) **the animal in each category which is not correct. Then add a different animal to each category in the list.**

1 Birds	2 Mammals	3 Reptiles
duck	eagle	snake
hippo	giraffe	bear
parrot	lion	crocodile
_____	_____	_____

3 ⭐⭐ **Read the descriptions and write the names of the animals from Exercise 1.**

1 This animal is a mammal. It usually lives in forests and cold places. It's very big and has a lot of hair.
_____bear_____

2 This animal lives in water in hot countries. It's a reptile with a big mouth and a lot of big teeth.
_____

3 This is a bird. It eats plants and it can swim and fly. It usually lives near water. _____

4 This animal likes cheese, but it doesn't like cats! It's usually gray and has a lot of babies.
_____

5 This animal eats meat. It doesn't have any legs. Some of them can kill other animals and sometimes people, too. _____

6 This is a very large sea mammal. It has a hole on the top of its head. _____

4 ⭐⭐ **Choose another animal from Exercise 1 and write a definition.**

This animal is _____

_____

_____

_____

Explore It! 🖱️

Guess the correct answer.

Which bird sometimes sleeps with an eye open?

a duck   b parrot   c eagle

Find another interesting fact about birds. Write a question and send it to a classmate in an email, or ask them it in the next class.

READING

Fact Files

1 ⭐ Read the fact file below and (circle) the correct answers.

1 Polar bears weigh …
   a about 360 kg.   b about 560 kg.

2 Polar bears live in …
   a the Arctic.   b the Antarctic.

3 Polar bears eat … of seal in a week.
   a about 35 kg   b about 55 kg

POLAR BEAR

Weight: about 360 kg
Habitat: the Arctic
Food: seals
Fact: Polar bears can smell a seal 32 km away! They can eat 55 kg of seal in a week.

2 ⭐ Read the article. What's special about the town of Churchill? _____

3 ⭐⭐ Read the article again and <u>underline</u> these words. Then check their meaning in a dictionary and complete the sentences.

> attack   escape   hunt   ~~ice~~   male   prison

1 In winter, there is ___ice___ on the river.

2 A female animal is a girl and a _____ is a boy.

3 People can go to _____ for killing an elephant.

4 Hungry lions are dangerous, and they sometimes _____ people.

5 Killer whales often _____ other mammals, like seals, at night.

6 The man saw the polar bear in the street and ran into a store to _____ .

Polar Bears Are in Town!

Churchill is a small town on the Hudson Bay in Canada. Every October, November, and December, it has some special visitors: polar bears! They can't hunt seals until it is colder and there is more ice, so they visit the town looking for food.

From October to December in 2016, there were 800 people living in Churchill and 10,000 tourists. The tourists were there to see the polar bears – there were more than 1,000 bears.

Some bears attack people, so the police ask people to be careful and to leave their cars open in town. Then people can jump inside if they need to escape an angry bear! To keep people safe, the police sometimes put angry bears in prison for a few days. Then they take them out of the town.

People in the town say the worst year was 1983. On November 29, a young male bear killed a man downtown. This was the first attack for many years. In 2013, a large bear attacked a man in the street. The bear was put in prison and the man went to the doctor, but he was fine after a few days.

4 ⭐⭐ Read the article again. Are the sentences *T* (true) or *F* (false)? Correct the false sentences.

1 Polar bears visit the town every August.
   F. Polar bears visit the town from October to December.

2 The polar bears go to the town because it's colder there.
   _____

3 When the polar bears are angry, people can hide in cars.
   _____

4 The polar bears that attack people go to prison.
   _____

5 ⭐⭐⭐ Answer the questions with your own ideas.

1 What do you think the polar bears eat in Churchill?
   _____

2 Do you think the food they eat in Churchill is good for them? Why / Why not?
   _____

GRAMMAR IN ACTION
Simple Past: *To Be, There Was/Were*

1 ⭐ (Circle) **the correct options.**

1 The polar bears *was* / (*were*) in Churchill in November because (*there wasn't*) / *there weren't* enough food for them to eat in the river.

2 In the past, the weather *was* / *were* always cold in November, and *there was* / *there were* a lot of ice on the river.

3 When it *was* / *were* colder, *there was* / *there were* seals for the polar bears to eat in the river.

4 In the past, *there was* / *there were* more ice because the temperatures *wasn't* / *weren't* as high.

2 ⭐ **Match the questions with the answers.**

1 Was it hotter in the past? ⬜   a   Yes, there were.

2 Were they wild animals? ⬜   b   No, there wasn't.

3 Was there ice in summer? ⬜   c   Yes, they were.

4 Were there seals? ⬜   d   No, it wasn't.

3 ⭐⭐ **Complete the text with *was(n't)*/*were(n't)*.**

Thousands of years ago, there were mammoths in Europe. They ¹ _were_ large mammals with very big tusks. They ² _____ very strong. They ³ _____ like the elephants we see today because they ⁴ _____ much bigger and had fur. The saber-toothed tiger also lived in Europe at the same time. It ⁵ _____ really a tiger. It ⁶ _____ a big cat. Its teeth ⁷ _____ very long, and it ⁸ _____ a very dangerous animal.

4 ⭐⭐ **Complete the text with the correct form of *there was* or *there were*.**

When I was a girl, I lived in South Africa. Around my house, ¹ _there wasn't_ a lot to do, but ² _____ a lot of animals to see because we lived next to a wildlife park. In my bedroom, ³ _____ a big window, and in the mornings, I could see a lot of animals. ⁴ _____ hippos in the water, and ⁵ _____ enormous elephants sleeping. ⁶ _____ always a big giraffe next to a tree and a strange bird sitting on the tree that looked angry! My favorite animals are tigers, but ⁷ _____ any tigers in the wildlife park. That's because there aren't any tigers in South Africa. ⁸ _____ a lot of time to see the animals because I was at school all day, but I remember all of them.

5 ⭐⭐ **Put the words in the correct order to complete the questions. Then write answers for you in your notebook.**

1 were / Where / on Saturday / you / ?
Where were you on Saturday?

2 your / favorite / six / animal / when / you / were / ?
What was _____

3 people / were / there / last year / your / class / in / ?
How many _____

4 in / 2011 / were / you / ?
How old _____

5 your town / in / were / you / when / young / a zoo / ?
Was there _____

6 ⭐⭐⭐ **Find out about an animal from the past, like mammoths or saber-toothed tigers. Write three sentences about them. Use *was* and *were*.**

_____

_____

_____

VOCABULARY AND LISTENING

Adjectives

1 ⭐ **Choose the correct letters to complete the adjectives.**

a	c	d	f̶	g	i	l	m	n	r	u	y

1 beauti _f_ ul
2 s__art
3 __ute
4 dan__erous

5 heav__
6 l__zy
7 wil__
8 no__sy

9 ti__y
10 la__ge
11 q__iet
12 __ong

2 ⭐⭐ **Complete the text with adjectives from Exercise 1.**

I have a ¹ _beautiful_ little cat. He has a pretty face, and I think he's really ² _____ . He's ³ _____ , too, and can do a lot of tricks. My mom likes him because he doesn't make a lot of noise like some pets. She says he's very ⁴ _____ . He can't run fast because his legs aren't very ⁵ _____ ! I prefer small pets because some of my friends' big pets are ⁶ _____ , and they make me nervous.

3 ⭐⭐⭐ **Which pets do your family or friends have? Use the adjectives and your own ideas to write four sentences.**

My best friend has a tiny mouse.

_____

_____

_____

A Class Discussion

🎧 **4** ⭐ **Listen to a teacher talking about wolves with her class. (Circle) the correct answers.**
7.01

1 The teacher is talking about wolves that live in an *American park* / *English zoo*.
2 There weren't any wolves there for *50* / *100* years.
3 There were about *6* / *100* wolves there last year.

🎧 **5** ⭐⭐ **Listen again and answer the questions. Remember the *Learn to Learn* tip: look for the question words and think about the answers before you listen.**
7.01

1 How does one student describe wolves?
   They are fast, dangerous, and smart.

2 Why weren't there any wolves in Yellowstone Park for 100 years?

   _____

   _____

3 How many wolves were in the park about 25 years ago?

   _____

4 Why was it difficult for the wolves at first?

   _____

   _____

5 Why is it difficult to see wolves in the park?

   _____

   _____

6 ⭐⭐⭐ **Which other wild animals do you think live in Yellowstone Park? Write some ideas below.**

_____

_____

_____

GRAMMAR IN ACTION
Simple Past: Regular and Irregular Verbs

1 ⭐ **Write the infinitive of these past tense verbs.**

1 had	_have_	5 heard	_____	9 shared	_____
2 slept	_____	6 saw	_____	10 wanted	_____
3 took	_____	7 became	_____	11 found	_____
4 looked	_____	8 gave	_____	12 went	_____

2 ⭐⭐ **Complete the sentences with the correct simple past form of the verbs in the box.**

> look   ~~not give~~   have   not want
> sleep   not find   see   not go

1 You _didn't give_ the donkey its food.

2 We _____ a lot of snakes at the wildlife park.

3 The horse _____ to eat my apple. It wasn't hungry.

4 They _____ for the cat in the yard, but they _____ him.

5 My dad _____ a parrot as a pet when he was a child.

6 The cat _____ out. She _____ on my bed all day.

3 ⭐⭐ **Write the words in the correct order to make sentences.**

1 park / years / The / 20 / safari / opened / ago

The safari park opened 20 years ago.

2 Crocodiles / killed / year / 1,000 / people / last

_____

3 bears / days / in town / ago, / Two / three / were / there

_____

4 blue / last / saw / whales / summer / They

_____

5 an / The / home / hour / cat / came / ago

_____

4 ⭐⭐⭐ **Complete the text with the simple past form of the verbs in parentheses.**

Flo, a dog from Northern Ireland, disappeared in October 2011. The Gallaghers, Flo's family, [1] _looked_ (look) for her, but they [2] _____ (not find) her. They were very sad. Then in 2014, a volunteer at the local animal hospital [3] _____ (hear) about a dog with no home. The dog [4] _____ (sleep) in an old building about ten miles from the Gallaghers' house. The volunteers at the hospital [5] _____ (not want) the dog to stay there. They [6] _____ (go) to find her. Soon the dog [7] _____ (have) a new home at the animal hospital, and they [8] _____ (share) photos of her on Facebook. The Gallagher family [9] _____ (see) the photos and [10] _____ (become) very excited – it was Flo! The next day they [11] _____ (take) her home. They [12] _____ (give) her a big dinner.

WRITING
A Biography

1 ⭐ Look at the photos and read the biography. Which animals did Jack help?

Jack Oliver

1 Jack Oliver was born in Australia ¹(in) / on 1978. His family started an animal sanctuary to give animals a safe place to live. ²When / At Jack was five, he found a three-meter snake in his yard! It was injured! Jack and his parents decided to take care of it. Jack helped at the sanctuary, and he became an animal expert.

2 Jack met his wife Alison ³on / in 2003. They had a daughter named Ava. ⁴In / On 2005, Jack started to make TV shows with a local TV channel. He filmed several series at his family's sanctuary. He also went to other countries to find and help injured animals. He helped to make them better and find a safe place for them to live. ⁵In / On September 25, 2012, Jack had an accident with a crocodile, but he survived.

3 Jack's wife and daughter help with his work. A few weeks ⁶when / ago, Ava found an injured duck and decided to take it to her father's sanctuary. She helped her father to take care of it. Ava wants to be an animal expert one day, just like her father!

2 ⭐⭐ (Circle) the correct prepositions (1–6) in the biography.

3 ⭐⭐ Read the biography again and write the events in the box in the timeline below.

| ~~born~~ | crocodile attack | found a snake |
| met Alison | TV shows |

←————————————————————————→

| 1978 | 1983 | 2003 | 2005 | 2012 |

1 _____born_____ 3 _____ 5 _____

2 _____ 4 _____

4 ⭐⭐ Match headings a–c with paragraphs 1–3.

a Now ☐
b Early life ☐
c Main events ☐

PLAN

5 ⭐⭐ Write a biography about a famous person who works with animals. Look for information on the Internet and create a timeline about his or her life. Use Exercise 3 to help you.

6 Decide what information to include in each paragraph. Use Exercise 4 to help you.

WRITE

7 ⭐⭐⭐ Write your biography. Remember to include three paragraphs, the simple past, and time expressions, and the *Useful Language* expressions (see Student's Book, p89).

CHECK

8 Do you ...
- give information from the timeline of your famous person?
- write about the events in their life in the correct order?

VOCABULARY

1 Complete the crossword. Use the pictures.

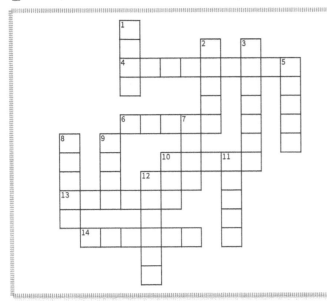

ACROSS →
4 6 10
13 14

DOWN ↓
1 2 3
5 7 8
9 11 12

2 Complete the sentences with an adjective from the box.

> beautiful cute dangerous heavy large
> lazy noisy quiet smart tiny wild

1 Kodiak brown bears are very _____ animals, but their babies are _____ – they are only about 23 cm long, and they weigh only 450 g.

2 Hippos are very _____ animals. They kill a lot of people.

3 My snake doesn't make much noise. He is very _____.

4 When blue whales are born, they weigh about 2,700 kg. That's _____!

5 Male lions are _____. They sleep, and the female lions hunt.

6 African gray parrots can learn 1,000 words. They are really _____.

7 Howler monkeys are very _____. You can hear them from 4 km away!

8 Baby lions look _____, but be careful! They are _____ animals, not pets, and can attack you.

9 Oh, I love looking at photos of tigers! I think tigers are really _____ animals.

GRAMMAR IN ACTION

3 Circle the correct options in the conversation.

A [1]*Was / Were* you at school yesterday?

B No, I [2]*wasn't / weren't.* [3]*There were / I was* on a school field trip to an aquarium.

A [4]*Was it / Was there* good?

B It was fantastic! There [5]*was / were* hundreds of different fish. My favorites [6]*were / was* the parrot fish and the clown fish. [7]*There was / It was* a dolphin area, too.

A [8]*Were there / There was* any sharks?

B Yes, [9]*they were / there were*, but there [10]*wasn't / weren't* time to go and see them. The aquarium's really big!

4 Complete the text with the simple past form of the verbs in parentheses.

Last year, I ¹_____ (want) a pet, but I ²_____ (not have) a lot of money, so I ³_____ (go) to an animal rescue center. At the center, I ⁴_____ (see) a lot of animals, but I ⁵_____ (not know) which one I ⁶_____ (like) best. Then I ⁷_____ (hear) a noise in a corner. A tiny white cat ⁸_____ (look) up at me with his big blue eyes. He was really cute. I ⁹_____ (take) him home, and he ¹⁰_____ (become) my best friend.

CUMULATIVE GRAMMAR

5 Complete the conversation with the missing words. (Circle) the correct options.

ISA Hi, Adela! How ¹_____ your weekend?

ADELA ²_____ really nice, thanks! On Saturday morning I ³_____ basketball with my team – we ⁴_____ our game.

ISA No way! Your team always wins!

ADELA I know, but it ⁵_____ fun to play, and we are still at the top of the league table. Anyway, on Saturday afternoon I ⁶_____ to a soccer match with my cousins and my uncle – my team ⁷_____ so I ⁸_____ really happy!

ISA Wow! Lucky you!

ADELA Yes, then on Sunday afternoon, I ⁹_____ my friends, and we went to the movies. ¹⁰_____ a great movie! The best part was the burger we ¹¹_____ in a restaurant near the theater after the movie. It was delicious!

ISA Really? Where's the restaurant?

ADELA On George Street. Let's go there now!

ISA

ADELA

1	a was	b are	c were
2	a There was	b There were	c It was
3	a plays	b did play	c played
4	a lost	b losed	c loses
5	a were	b weren't	c was
6	a was	b go	c went
7	a wins	b won	c win
8	a wasn't	b aren't	c was
9	a meet	b meeted	c met
10	a It was	b It weren't	c It wasn't
11	a eat	b eated	c ate

8 What did you find?

VOCABULARY
Places in Town

1 ⭐ **Look at the photos and complete the words for places.**

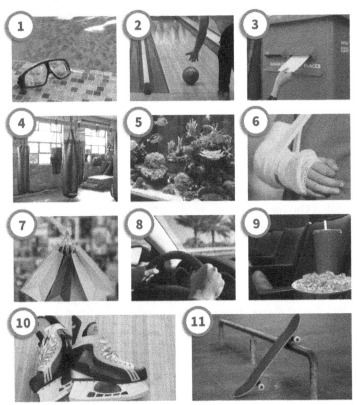

1 s w i m m i n g
  p o o l
2 b _ _ _ _ _ _ _
  a _ _ _ _ _
3 p _ _ _ _
  o _ _ _ _ _
4 g _ _ _
5 a _ _ _ _ _ _ _
6 h _ _ _ _ _ _ _

7 s _ _ _ _ _ _ _
  m _ _ _ _
8 p _ _ _ _ _ _
  l _ _ _
9 m _ _ _ _ _
  t _ _ _ _ _ _
10 i _ _ _ r _ _ _ _
11 s _ _ _ _ _
   p _ _ _ _

2 ⭐ **Look at the words in Exercise 1. How many are compound nouns?** _____

3 ⭐ **Write a place from Exercise 1.**

1 I went there when I fell off my bike. ___hospital___
2 It was cold in there, but we wore gloves and it was fun! _____
3 We went there to buy some clothes and gifts.
  _____
4 I went there to send a letter. _____

4 ⭐⭐ **Complete the text with the places from Exercise 1.**

My friend Edie lives in a small town. She always goes to the city to buy her clothes because there isn't a ¹ __shopping mall__ in her town. There's a library with a lot of good books, and a ² _____ to send letters, but nothing else. There isn't a ³ _____ to watch movies! I live in a big town, and there's everything we need. I go to the ⁴ _____ to play tennis and take swimming classes at the ⁵ _____. In December, I love ice skating at the ⁶ _____ and going bowling at the ⁷ _____. My town also has a ⁸ _____ – I was there last year when I broke my arm! But my favorite place is downtown – it's an ⁹ _____ with a lot of fish. My dad takes me there sometimes and leaves the car in a big ¹⁰ _____. After that, I usually go skateboarding in a cool ¹¹ _____ nearby.

Explore It! 🖱

Guess the correct answer.
The first bowling alley opened in …
a London in 1889.   b New York in 1840.

Find another interesting fact about a place from Exercise 1 in your country. Write a question and send it to a classmate in an email, or ask them it in the next class.

READING

An Online Travel Article

1 ⭐ Look at the photos and read the article. Which photo (1–3) is the article <u>not</u> about? _____

2 ⭐⭐ Read the article and <u>underline</u> these words. Check their meaning in a dictionary and then complete the sentences.

> believe   belong   case   ~~scuba diving~~   social media

1 I love swimming, but I prefer _scuba diving_ underwater.

2 Matt has a blog and shares his videos on _____.

3 I can't _____ it! Our birthdays are on the same day!

4 Keep the camera safe. Put it in its _____.

5 This cap isn't mine. Does it _____ to you?

3 ⭐⭐ Read the article again. Put the events in the correct order (1–8).

a Serina saw the photos on social media. ☐

b Serina went scuba diving. [1]

c The teacher put a message on social media. ☐

d The teacher looked at the photos on the camera. ☐

e Some children found a camera on the beach. ☐

f Serina lost her camera. ☐

g The children and their teacher took the camera back to school. ☐

h Thousands of people shared the message. ☐

4 ⭐⭐⭐ Imagine you are Serina. Write a thank-you note to Mr. Park Lee and his class. Write at least four sentences.

Dear Mr. Park Lee and students: ...

_____

_____

_____

_____

_____

Lost Under the Ocean

In March 2018, a class from Mount Elementary School in Su'ao, Taiwan, went to clean the beach. They found a camera in an underwater case. They didn't know it was a camera at first because the case had things from the ocean all over it. They showed their teacher, Mr. Park Lee. He opened the case. Inside was a digital camera, and no sea water!

The class took the camera back to school. Everyone had questions: Did it work? Were there any photos in it? Did it belong to someone from Su'ao? Could they find him or her? The camera worked! Mr. Park Lee looked at the photos. They showed fish and people underwater, and streets in Japan. Mr. Lee put some photos with a message in Chinese and Japanese on social media. He asked people to share the message with their friends. In the next 24 hours, thousands of people saw the message. One of them was Serina Tsubakihara, a Japanese student. She couldn't believe it – they were her photos!

Serina went scuba diving near Okinawa, in Japan, in September 2015. She lost her camera there. It was in the ocean for more than two years and traveled 250 kilometers to Taiwan!

GRAMMAR IN ACTION
Simple Past: Questions

1 ⭐ **Match questions 1–5 with answers a–e.**

1 Did Sam find his hat? `c`
2 Did the students go to the bowling alley? ☐
3 Did you and Dana finish your project? ☐
4 Did the ice rink close at six o'clock? ☐
5 Did Rosa go to the movies? ☐

a Yes, we did.
b No, she didn't.
c Yes, he did.
d Yes, it did.
e No, they didn't.

2 ⭐ **Answer the questions for you. Mark (✓) the correct column.**

Yesterday, did you ...	Yes, I did.	No, I didn't.
... have a big breakfast?		
... play any sports?		
... go to the movies?		
... visit a family member?		
... hang out with friends after school?		

3 ⭐⭐ **Write the words in the correct order to make simple past questions.**

1 Alex / to / post office / Did / go / the / ?
   Did Alex go to the post office?
2 buy / a / Clara / bag / new / Did / ?
   _____
3 Did / time / they / good / have / a / ?
   _____
4 aquarium / the / Did / enjoy / you / ?
   _____
5 your / Did / to / parents / walk / restaurant / the / ?
   _____

4 ⭐⭐ **Write simple past questions. Do you know the answers?**

1 Shakespeare / write *Romeo and Juliet* / ?
   Did Shakespeare write Romeo and Juliet?
2 Marie Curie / win a Nobel Prize / ?
   _____
3 Picasso / paint the *Mona Lisa* / ?
   _____
4 Columbus / discover Australia / ?
   _____
5 Emma Watson / work in the movie *Frozen* / ?
   _____

5 ⭐⭐⭐ **Complete the conversation with simple past questions. Use the words in parentheses and the <u>underlined</u> verbs.**

MOM	Hi! ¹*Did you have a good match*? (you / good match)
RYAN	No, we <u>had</u> a terrible match.
MOM	Oh, no! ² _____? (your team)
RYAN	Yes. We <u>lost</u> 5–3.
MOM	³ _____ (you / a goal)
RYAN	No, I didn't <u>score</u> this time.
MOM	What about Henry? ⁴ _____? (he)
RYAN	No, he didn't <u>play</u>. He fell off his skateboard the other day.
MOM	Oh, no. ⁵ _____? (he / anything)
RYAN	Luckily, he didn't <u>break</u> his leg. He just hurt it.
MOM	Good! ⁶ _____ after the match? (you / a snack)
RYAN	Yes, I <u>had</u> some chocolate. That was the best part!

VOCABULARY AND LISTENING
Personal Possessions

1 ⭐ **Complete the definitions with the words in the box.**

> bus pass   camera   ~~headphones~~   ID card
> keys   money   passport   phone
> portable charger

We use …

1 ___headphones___ to listen to music.

2 our _____ and _____ to show who we are.

3 _____ to buy things.

4 _____ to open a door.

5 a _____ to travel on public transportation.

6 a _____ to text or talk to someone.

7 a _____ to take photos or make videos.

8 a _____ to keep our phone, tablet, or laptop working.

2 ⭐⭐ **Complete the text with words from Exercise 1.**

Home   News   **Blog**   Lifestyle   🔍

I had a bad day on Tuesday. I couldn't take the bus home because I couldn't find my ¹___bus pass___. Then I couldn't get into our apartment because I didn't have my ²_____. I used my ³_____ to text my mom, but she was at the doctor's! I went to the library to do some homework on my laptop, but it had no battery power and the ⁴_____ was at home. I had some ⁵_____ in my pocket, so I bought a drink at the café. My sister loses things, too. Last July, she lost her ⁶_____ on vacation and couldn't take any photos. Then she left her ⁷_____ on a bus, so she couldn't listen to music on her phone. What a family!

A Radio Interview

🎧 3 8.01 ⭐ **Look at the photos and answer the questions with your own ideas. Then listen and check your answers.**

1 What did Sabina lose? _____

2 Where did she find it/them? _____

🎧 4 8.01 ⭐⭐ **Listen again. Underline and correct one mistake in each sentence.**

1 The tickets <u>weren't</u> Sabina's birthday present.
___were___

2 Sabina asked her mom for help.
_____

3 Sabina's friend put the envelope in the trash can. _____

4 Sabina's CD wasn't in her room. _____

5 She didn't go to the concert. _____

🎧 5 8.01 ⭐⭐ **Listen again and complete the sentences.**

1 The radio show today is about
_____.

2 Sabina's best friend never _____.

3 The questions helped Sabina
_____.

GRAMMAR IN ACTION
Simple Past: *Wh-* Questions

1 ⭐ **Complete the questions with the question words in the box.**

> How much   What   When   ~~Where~~   Who

1 A: _____Where_____ did you buy your new headphones?   B: Around the corner.
2 A: _____ did they cost?   B: About $20.
3 A: _____ did you do last weekend?   B: I went to the movies.
4 A: _____ did you go with?   B: My cousin.
5 A: _____ did you get that camera?   B: Last week, for my birthday.

2 ⭐⭐ **Write simple past questions. Then match them with answers a–e.**

1 What / you / do / last night?   [e]
   What did you do last night?

2 How / you / get / to school / today?   ☐
   _____

3 Who / you / sit / with in class / yesterday?   ☐
   _____

4 Where / you / go / last weekend?   ☐
   _____

5 What time / get up / on Sunday?   ☐
   _____

a My best friend.
b Really late! At 11 o'clock!
c I caught the bus.
d I went to the aquarium with my friends.
e ~~I watched TV and read a book.~~

3 ⭐⭐⭐ **Complete questions in the conversation with the simple past. Use the answers to help you.**

ANA   Hey! I went to a baseball game in Chicago.
ROB   Wow! When ¹ _____ did you go _____?
ANA   I went last weekend, on Saturday.
ROB   Who ² _____?
ANA   I went with my family and my American cousin, Martin.
ROB   Who ³ _____?
ANA   I sat with Martin. He told me everything about the game.

4 ⭐⭐⭐ **Think about an interesting event you went to. Write the questions. Then answer them.**

1 where / go?   _Where did you go?_
2 when / go?   _____
3 who / go with?   _____
4 how / feel?   _____

I went …
_____
_____
_____

ROB   What ⁴ _____?
ANA   I ate a big burger!
ROB   How ⁵ _____?
ANA   We went home by bus.
ROB   What time ⁶ _____?
ANA   I can't remember, but I know we got home really late!

WRITING
A Blog Post

1 ⭐ **Read the blog post. What problem started Bruno's bad day?** (Circle) **the correct answer.**

a His camera didn't work.

b His sister's camera didn't work.

c His parents' car didn't work.

● ● ●

HOME **ABOUT ME** ARCHIVE FOLLOW

BRUNO'S BIG BLOG

A Bad Day on the Weekend

1 Last Saturday, it was my sister's birthday. We gave her a camera, but it didn't work. My mom and dad decided to go to the shopping mall to exchange it, so we all got ready.

2 When we got into the car, it didn't work, so we decided to take the bus. But it got worse! It started raining, so we arrived wet and cold at the store. Awful. 😱

3 At the store, the sales assistant asked for the receipt to exchange the camera, and guess what? My parents didn't have it … so my dad went back home to get it. After an hour, he came back, and my sister got her new camera.

4 It was lunchtime, and we were really hungry, so we had lunch in the shopping mall. But when my parents wanted to pay, they couldn't find their wallets … they were at home! 😫

5 When did you have a bad day on a weekend? What happened? Tell me!

2 ⭐⭐ **Read the blog again. Put the events in the correct order (1–5).**

a Bruno's dad went back home. ☐

b They needed a receipt for the camera. ☐

c They took the bus to the shopping mall. ☐

d The family car didn't work. [1]

e Bruno's parents couldn't pay for lunch. ☐

3 ⭐⭐ **Join the sentences with *so*.**

1 It was my sister's birthday. We bought her a phone.

It was my sister's birthday, so we bought her a phone.

2 The phone didn't work. We decided to exchange it.

_____

3 My dad showed the receipt. My sister got her new phone.

_____

4 My parents couldn't find their wallets. They couldn't pay for lunch.

_____

4 Read the blog post again. Match topics a–e with paragraphs 1–5.

a what happened next ☐

b what day it was and how it started [1]

c what happened later ☐

d sign off and ask questions ☐

e the end of the bad day ☐

PLAN

5 ⭐⭐ **Write a blog post about a bad day on the weekend. Make notes about your bad day. Think about the answers to these questions.**

When did the bad day start?
What problems did you and your family/friends have?
When and where did each problem happen?
What did you do? What did the other people do?
How did you feel?

6 Decide what information to include in each paragraph. Use the information in Exercise 4 to help you.

WRITE

7 ⭐⭐⭐ **Write your blog post. Remember to include four paragraphs, the simple past for the questions at the end, and the expressions from the *Useful Language* box (see Student's Book, p101).**

CHECK

8 Do you …

• use a title for your blog post?

• use *so* to join ideas and explain the results?

• say how you felt on your bad day?

VOCABULARY

1 Where did Tim go last week? Match the sentences with the words in the box. (Circle) the four extra words.

> aquarium   bowling alley   gym
> hospital   ice rink   movie theater
> parking lot   post office   shopping mall
> skate park   swimming pool

1 He mailed a letter to Ben. _____

2 He saw a basketball game. _____

3 He visited his sick uncle. _____

4 He saw an amazing movie. _____

5 He bought a new pair of jeans. _____

6 He saw a lot of dolphins! _____

7 He dived into the water. _____

2 Which four places from Exercise 1 didn't Tim go to?

_____ _____

_____ _____

3 Complete the sentences with the words in the box.

> camera   concert tickets   headphones
> keys   money   passport   phone   tablet

1 I don't have any _____ to buy a drink.

2 You need your _____ to travel to a different country.

3 These _____ don't work. I can't hear anything!

4 These days, everyone has a _____ to text and call people.

5 It's easy to use a _____ . You just touch the screen and it works!

6 Let's buy _____ to see Katy Perry.

7 Henry doesn't use his phone to take photos. He uses his _____ .

8 Where are the _____ to open the door?

GRAMMAR IN ACTION

4 Complete the questions and short answers with the simple past. Use the verbs in parentheses.

ASHLEY ¹ _____ you _____ (go) to the bowling alley yesterday, Max?

MAX   Yes, I ² _____ .

ASHLEY ³ _____ you _____ (meet) Maddie there?

MAX   No, I ⁴ _____ . I was with Alex and Elena.

ASHLEY Cool! And ⁵ _____ you _____ (have) a good time?

MAX   No, we ⁶ _____ . Alex dropped the bowling ball on his foot!

ASHLEY Oh, no! Poor Alex! ⁷ _____ his parents _____ (take) him to the hospital?

MAX   Yes, they ⁸ _____ .

ASHLEY Was his foot OK? ⁹ _____ he _____ (break) it?

MAX   No, he ¹⁰ _____ . He was very lucky!

5 Write simple past questions.

1 What / you / do / last night?

2 How / your dad / get to work / this morning?

3 What time / you / get home / after school?

4 Who / you / see / yesterday?

5 Where / you / go / last weekend?

6 How / you / feel / after the exam?

CUMULATIVE GRAMMAR

6 Complete the conversation with the missing words. (Circle) the correct options.

BRENDA Hi, Theo. Where ¹_____ go yesterday?

THEO I ²_____ to the ice rink to watch my brother.

BRENDA ³_____ go ice skating, too?

THEO No! I don't ⁴_____ ice skating. I think it's dangerous!

BRENDA Yes, me too! The first time I ⁵_____ it, I nearly ⁶_____ my leg!

THEO The other problem is that ⁷_____ usually a lot of people on the ice.

BRENDA Yes, you're right! ⁸_____ does your brother go?

THEO He ⁹_____ every week for about three hours. He says he wants to be the ¹⁰_____ ice skater in town!

BRENDA ¹¹_____ you at the ice rink all day yesterday?

THEO Yes, but he ¹²_____ me out for dinner afterward!

1 a do you	b did you	c you did
2 a go	b went	c goes
3 a Did you	b You	c Were you
4 a like	b likes	c liked
5 a try	b tries	c tried
6 a broke	b break	c breaks
7 a there is	b there are	c there were
8 a How often	b How many	c How
9 a practice	b practices	c practiced
10 a good	b better	c best
11 a Did	b Was	c Were
12 a take	b took	c takes

9 What makes a great vacation?

VOCABULARY
Outdoor Life

1 ⭐ Look at the pictures. Complete the activities with the words and phrases in the box.

> a compass   a fire   a map   a shelter
> fish   ~~food and water~~   fruit
> over a campfire   plants   wood

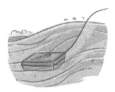

1 find _food and water_

6 cook _____

2 pick _____

7 identify _____

3 light _____

8 catch _____

4 collect _____

9 build _____

5 use _____

10 read _____

2 ⭐⭐ Match the sentences with activities from Exercise 1.

a You do this before nighttime. You sleep there. ⑨

b You need to do this before you light a fire. ☐

c You need to find trees with apples, pears, etc. to do this. ☐

d You use this to see where places are. ☐

e You use this to know which way to go. ☐

f You do this to keep warm and to cook. ☐

g You do this when you are hungry or thirsty. ☐

3 ⭐⭐ Complete the text with the correct form of the verbs from Exercise 1.

> I often go to the mountains with my family. When we get there, some of us ¹ _collect_ wood for the fire and others ² _____ a shelter. Next, we all go to ³_____ water and ⁴_____ fish for lunch. My dad always ⁵_____ the fish over a campfire. It can take a long time to ⁶_____ the fire if the wood is wet. In the afternoon, we go for a walk to ⁷_____ plants. I write their names in my notebook. We sometimes ⁸_____ fruit, too. We ⁹_____ a compass in the mountains because it's easy to get lost!

4 ⭐⭐⭐ Write about one or more outdoor activities that you do on vacation. Look at Exercise 3 to help you.

_____

_____

_____

_____

Explore It! 🖱

Guess the correct answer.

In this country, students have the longest summer break from school in Europe. They get 13 weeks! Which country is it?

a Italy   b Germany   c Portugal

Find another interesting fact about how people spend their free time in your country. Write a question and send it to a classmate in an email, or ask them it in the next class.

READING
A Pamphlet

ADVENTURE TRIPS

FIND AN ADVENTURE TRIP FOR YOU THIS SUMMER!

You'll learn new things and have a lot of fun! Join us on one of our three Adventure Trips. Read and choose the best one for you!

1. WHITE WATER KAYAKING TRIP (THREE DAYS)

Day 1: Meet your instructors and practice on white water.

Day 2: Learn how to use a compass and choose the best part of the river for your kayak.

Day 3: Follow the fast water and show your instructors how good you are!

We'll also teach you to build a shelter and help you collect wood for a campfire.

2. MOUNTAIN CLIMBING TRIP (FIVE DAYS)

Days 1–2: Walk five kilometers in the mountains each day with your guide. Learn how to identify plants and pick the right fruit to eat!

Days 3–5: Spend three days mountain climbing. Learn how to read a map and help each other.

You won't get much time to sit down! But you'll become the best mountain climber!

3. WATER AND COUNTRY TRIP (SIX DAYS)

Day 1: Learn how to catch fish in the river and then cook them over a campfire!

Days 2–3: Travel along the river in a kayak and work as a team.

Days 4–6: Leave the water to go horseback riding in the country with your guides!

You won't be bored on this trip. We'll play fun games, and you'll make good friends!

WHAT ARE YOU WAITING FOR?
CHOOSE THE BEST ADVENTURE TRIP FOR YOU!

You'll learn new sports and skills, meet new people, and have a great time!

For more information and booking details, visit our website.

We'll give you breakfast and lunch, but sometimes … you'll need to find your own dinner!

---

1 ☆ **Read the pamphlet. Then complete the sentences with the phrases in the box.**

> mountain climbing   water and country
> white water kayaking

1 You can learn how to read a map and identify plants on the _____ trip.

2 You can learn how to cook your own food over a campfire on the _____ trip.

3 You can learn how to use a compass on the _____ trip.

2 ☆☆ **Read the pamphlet again and <u>underline</u> these words. Then check their meaning in a dictionary and complete the sentences.**

> white water   ~~river~~   follow   guides   spend

1 There are a lot of fish in that __river__.

2 The water in a river that moves very quickly is called _____.

3 Our mountain _____ showed us some good places to climb.

4 Don't walk alone in the forest. Always _____ the instructor.

5 I need to _____ more time learning how to build a shelter!

3 ☆☆☆ **Answer the questions.**

1 On Trip 1, who do you meet on Day 1?
your instructors

2 On which day do you use a compass?
_____

3 On Trip 2, how far do you walk on Day 1?
_____

4 What things can you learn on Trip 2?
_____
_____

5 On Trip 3, when do you do water activities?
_____

4 ☆☆☆ **Answer the questions with your own ideas.**

1 Which trip is the most exciting? Why?
_____

2 Which trip is the most difficult? Why?
_____

GRAMMAR IN ACTION
Future with *Will/Won't*

1 ⭐ (Circle) the correct options.

1 The climbing trip *be* / *(will be)* a lot of fun.
It *not will* / *won't* be boring.

2 We *won't* / *not will* make our own lunch. The instructors *make will* / *will make* it.

3 **A:** *Will you* / *You will* go on the kayaking trip?
B: Yes, *I'll* / *I will*.

4 **A:** *Will* / *Will not* the instructors make dinner for you?
B: No, they *not will* / *won't*.

2 ⭐⭐ Write sentences with *I'll* or *I won't*.

1 (✓) learn how to catch fish
   I'll learn how to catch fish.

2 (✗) get bored
   _____

3 (✓) go in a kayak
   _____

4 (✗) stay for two weeks
   _____

5 (✓) walk six kilometers
   _____

6 (✓) cook food over a campfire
   _____

3 ⭐⭐ Complete the email with the correct form of *will* and the verbs in parentheses.

● ● ●

Hi Victoria,

I got back a few hours ago from my family camping trip. It was OK, but my sister says she ¹ __won't go__ (not go) again. She also ² _____ (not sleep) in a shelter again! She says she ³ _____ (go) with her friends on a beach vacation because it ⁴ _____ (be) sunny and they ⁵ _____ (not do) anything all day – just sleep and swim! She's 18 now, so I guess we ⁶ _____ (not be) together next summer. I ⁷ _____ (miss) her! How was your vacation?

4 ⭐⭐ Write the words in the correct order to make questions. Then answer the questions for you in your notebook.

1 with your family / Will / this year / you / go on vacation / ?
   Will you go on vacation with your family this year?

2 you / Will / see / on the weekend / your best friend / ?
   _____

3 tomorrow / will / you / do / What / ?
   _____

4 this summer / go / you / Where / will / ?
   _____

5 will / you / Who / next week / see / ?
   _____

6 go shopping / you / Will / tomorrow / ?
   _____

5 ⭐⭐⭐ You are going on one of the adventure trips from the pamphlet on p73. Make four predictions about it with *will/won't*.

1 I'll make new friends.

2 _____

3 _____

4 _____

5 _____

VOCABULARY AND LISTENING
Vacations

1 ⭐ **Complete the accommodation words in the spidergram with the missing vowels.**

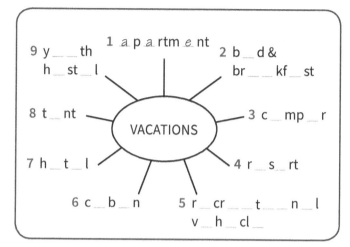

1 a p a r t m e nt
2 b _ d &
br _ _ kf _ st
3 c _ mp _ r
4 r _ s _ rt
5 r _ cr _ _ t _ _ n _ l
v _ h _ cl _
6 c _ b _ n
7 h _ t _ l
8 t _ nt
9 y _ _ th
h _ st _ l

VACATIONS

2 ⭐⭐ **Complete the text with words from Exercise 1.**

My family and I want to go on vacation, but everyone wants to stay in a different place! My dad wants to stay in a ¹hotel_____, but my mom prefers a ²b_____ & b_____. My brother loves moving from place to place, so he thinks a ³r_____ v_____ is perfect! My grandma wants a little house like a ⁴c_____, but my dad says that's very small. My aunt showed me a picture of an amazing city ⁵a_____. It looks great, but I want to stay in a ⁶y_____ h_____ — it's the best place to make friends!

A Conversation

🎧 **3** ⭐ **Listen to the conversation. Where will the girls spend their summer vacations?** (Circle) **the correct answer.**
9.01

a in a cabin   b at home   c in Canada

🎧 **4** ⭐⭐ **Listen again. Match the phrases with the people in the box.**
9.01

> aunt and uncle   Camila   ~~parents~~   Tara

1 on vacation in another country ___parents___
2 a lot of fun _____
3 at home with her parents in the summer
_____
4 invites her friend to do an outdoor activity
_____

🎧 **5** ⭐⭐ **Listen again and answer the questions.**
9.01

1 How will Camila's parents travel around Canada?
  in an RV
2 Who will be with Camila for two weeks?
_____
3 Whose parents have a vacation cabin?
_____
4 What will Tara's parents do in July and August?
_____
5 Why does Camila ask Tara to stay with her?
_____
6 Why doesn't Tara like camping?
_____

6 ⭐⭐⭐ **Your parents are going on vacation, and you will stay at home with someone else from your family. Make a spidergram with positive/ negative things about this.**

GRAMMAR IN ACTION
Present Continuous for Future

1 ☆ **Match 1–6 with a–f.**

1 My mom's working on Saturday. | c |
2 Are you watching the match tomorrow? | ☐ |
3 Mario isn't playing tennis after school. | ☐ |
4 Are your cousins arriving soon? | ☐ |
5 We're going on a field trip tomorrow. | ☐ |
6 How are you getting to the gym? | ☐ |

a We're visiting a museum.
b My dad's driving me.
c ~~She's going to a meeting.~~
d He's going to the dentist.
e No, I'm not. I'm studying.
f Yes, they are. On Sunday.

2 ☆☆ **Write sentences with the present continuous.**

1 We / go / to the beach / on the weekend
   We're going to the beach on the weekend.

2 Debra / not have / a birthday party / this year
   _____

3 My grandparents / fly / to Italy / in August
   _____

4 you / have / lunch / at a restaurant / on Sunday / ?
   _____

5 We / not do / anything special / this weekend
   _____

6 How / she / get / to work / today / ?
   _____

3 ☆☆ **Complete the conversation with the present continuous form of the verbs in parentheses.**

CARLA What ¹ *are you doing* (you / do) in the
summer?
NICO In July, I ² _____ (go) to a
summer camp in the mountains.
CARLA That sounds fun! ³ _____
(you / sleep) in a tent?
NICO No, I ⁴ _____ (not camp).
We ⁵ _____ (stay) in cabins.
CARLA What ⁶ _____ (your parents /
do)?
NICO They ⁷ _____ (start)
their vacation in August. They
⁸ _____ (meet) me at the
summer camp, and we
⁹ _____ (drive) across the
country in an RV.

Be Going To

4 ☆ <u>Underline</u> **and correct one mistake in each sentence.**

1 <u>We going</u> to visit the water park.   *We're going*
2 Are you going see the new movie?   _____
3 I'm not go to buy a camera.   _____
4 They're going living in the country.   _____
5 Mia isn't to go swimming after school. _____
6 Leo going to learn to skateboard.   _____

5 ☆☆☆ **Write questions with the present continuous or** *be going to*. **Then answer the questions for you.**

1 What / do / this weekend? (present continuous)
   What are you doing this weekend?
   _____

2 What / do / tonight? (present continuous)
   _____

3 What TV shows / watch / this week? (*be going to*)
   _____

4 How / celebrate / your birthday / this year? (*be going to*)
   _____

WRITING
An Email

1 ⭐ **Read the email. How does Paige know Ava?**

_____

2 ⭐⭐ (Circle) **the correct prepositions (1–10) in the email.**

● ● ●

Hi Ava,

1 Thanks for your email. I'm really excited you're coming to stay with us in New Zealand ¹*on* / (*in*) January! 👏 We'll have a great time! You'll enjoy Mission Bay and seeing our friends from elementary school again.

2 Here are the arrangements. ²*On* / *In* Friday, Mom and I are meeting you ³*at* / *on* the airport in Auckland. Then we're going to have a night ⁴*in* / *at* home, and my dad's cooking. You're sleeping with me ⁵*in* / *at* my room. We can talk about your new life in Australia and compare our schools! 😊

3 ⁶*In* / *On* Saturday, we're going to the beach. 🌞 It'll be hot, so we'll go swimming. Hayley, Lily, and Ryan from our elementary school are coming, too! ⁷*In* / *On* the evening, we're going to have dinner ⁸*on* / *at* my favorite restaurant. Then ⁹*on* / *at* Sunday, we're going to Te Urewera National Park for four days. We're staying ¹⁰*in* / *on* a nice cabin. There are beautiful lakes and birds. What do you think?

4 It'll be great to see you again! Is there anything you would like to do? Let me know!

See you soon, 👍

Paige XX

---

3 **Match topics a–d with paragraphs 1–4.**

a end the email

b respond to your friend's last email ☐

c describe the first day ☐

d describe the weekend ☐

(paragraph box for a: [4])

4 ⭐⭐ **Read the email again. Are the sentences *T* (true) or *F* (false)?**

1 Ava is traveling to Auckland by car. ___F

2 Ava and Paige are sleeping in the same room. ___

3 They're spending one day at the beach. ___

4 They're having dinner at home on Saturday evening. ___

5 At Te Urewera National Park, they're not staying in a hotel. ___

PLAN

5 ⭐⭐ **Write an email to a friend from elementary school about plans for their visit. Your friend now lives in another place and is coming to stay with you. Make notes about these things for your email:**

> your arrangements
> things you intend to do
> predictions about what will happen
> the place where you are meeting them

6 ⭐⭐ **Decide what information to include in each paragraph. Use the information in Exercise 3 to help you.**

WRITE

7 ⭐⭐⭐ **Write your email. Remember to include four paragraphs, *will*, *be going to*, and the present continuous for future, and expressions from the *Useful Language* box (see Student's Book, p113).**

CHECK

8 **Do you ...**

- include an arrangement and a prediction for the weekend and the week ahead?
- make predictions about what will or won't happen?
- tell your friend where you are going to meet them?

VOCABULARY

1 (Circle) the correct verb.

1 *catch / build* a shelter

2 *light / cook* a fire

3 *build / pick* fruit

4 *catch / light* fish

5 *use / cook* over a campfire

6 *collect / build* wood

7 *read / collect* a map

8 *build / identify* plants

2 Find nine words for accommodation in the word search. Then match them with sentences 1–9 below.

C	T	E	N	T	Y	B	E	G	F	B
A	B	R	L	H	O	C	I	J	N	E
M	C	E	O	I	U	E	O	G	C	D
P	A	S	M	K	T	G	U	B	T	&
E	I	O	E	M	H	O	T	E	L	B
R	T	R	Y	R	H	M	E	V	L	R
V	F	T	X	C	O	X	T	G	A	E
K	A	Z	C	W	S	N	A	S	A	A
N	A	P	A	R	T	M	E	N	T	K
J	O	G	B	X	E	Q	M	R	B	F
K	P	E	I	O	L	T	X	S	C	A
R	M	V	N	A	A	R	V	N	A	S
O	U	H	O	H	I	D	G	Y	S	T

1 This can be a problem in the rain. _____

2 A place where young people normally stay. _____

3 You can drive with your bed in this! _____

4 A small country house. _____

5 You can drive this. _____

6 You only stay here to sleep and eat in the morning. _____

7 This is in a building, often in a city. _____

8 An expensive one has five stars. _____

9 A ski or beach vacation destination. _____

GRAMMAR IN ACTION

3 Complete the conversation with the correct form of *will* or *won't*. Use the verbs in parentheses.

● ● ●

| Wall | Find friends | Chat |

IAN 1h ago
1 _____ (we / sleep) in tents?

GUIDE 1h ago
No, you 2 _____ (not sleep) in a tent. You
3 _____ (stay) in a resort. Every night, we
4 _____ (cook) dinner over a campfire.

IAN 1h ago
Sounds fun. What activities 5 _____
(we / do)?

GUIDE 1h ago
You 6 _____ (go) walking and climbing
in the mountains. We 7 _____ (teach) you
how to read a map, so you 8 _____
(not get) lost. It 9 _____ (be) fantastic.
You 10 _____ (not forget) the
experience, I'm sure!

4 Complete the email with the present continuous form of the verbs in parentheses.

● ● ●

Hi Sonia,

What 1 _____ (you / do)
this summer? In July, my parents
2 _____ (work), so Paul and
I 3 _____ (not plan) anything
special. He 4 _____ (go) to a
soccer camp, and I 5 _____
(stay) with my grandparents. Then in
August we 6 _____ (fly) to
Mexico for a family vacation. My parents
7 _____ (rent) an
apartment at the beach, and then we
8 _____ (drive) up to the
mountains in a camper. I'm very excited!

5 Write sentences about the pictures. Use the correct form of *be going to* and the phrases in the box.

> climb a mountain   get on a plane   go horseback riding
> play volleyball   sleep in a tent   walk in the forest

1 He _____

2 She _____

3 He _____

4 She _____

5 They _____

6 They _____

CUMULATIVE GRAMMAR

6 Complete the text with the missing words. (Circle) the correct options.

I had ¹_____ amazing vacation of my life last year. ²_____ go? I went to Peru on ³_____ adventure vacation! We built a shelter to sleep in and learned ⁴_____ new things, like how to catch fish and find fruit to eat in the forest. We played ⁵_____ sports, too. They were fun! I loved ⁶_____ kayaking, but I ⁷_____ horseback riding. It was frightening! I have a lot of photos. Would you like to see ⁸_____ ?

This vacation was ⁹_____ than my vacation two years ago. Now I ¹⁰_____ a lot of new friends. At the moment, we ¹¹_____ emails to each other to get together this year. I can't ¹²_____ !

	a	b	c
1	the more	most	the most
2	Where did I	What I did	When did I
3	some	a	an
4	much	a lot	a lot of
5	an	any	some
6	going	go	do
7	wasn't enjoy	didn't enjoy	not enjoy
8	them	they	it
9	better	the best	good
10	has	had	have
11	writing	're writing	write
12	to wait	wait	waiting

EXAM TIPS: Reading Skills

Reading: Multiple Matching

You will read three short texts about three different people.
They are all about the same topic. The title tells you what the topic is. There are seven questions.
To answer the question, you need to choose the correct answer, A, B, or C.

Example:

	Tim	Tom	Ted
Which person did a lot of sports at school?	*A*	*B*	*C*

Exam Guide: Multiple Matching

- Start by reading the title of the text so you know what the topic is.

- Read all the questions carefully and <u>underline</u> the important words. This helps when you look for the same information in the texts.

  Example:

  Which person did <u>a lot of sports</u> at <u>school</u>?

- Now read the three texts for the first time without stopping. Maybe you see information similar to the questions, but read to the end.

- Now read the first question again. Then look at the texts to find which person says this. Maybe you remember something from one of the texts, so go to that text first to check. If not, just read from the beginning until you find what you need.

- When you find the correct answer, <u>underline</u> the words in the text with the same meaning as the question. Write the number of the question next to the part you <u>underlined</u>. Then choose your answer, A, B, or C.

  Example:

  When I was a teenager, <u>I was on the school hockey, track and field, and swimming teams</u>.

- Then read the next question and do the same until you finish.

- You don't lose points for a wrong answer, so always choose a letter, even if you're not sure.

REMEMBER!

When you look for the answer, remember that the words in the question are probably different from the words in the text, but the meaning is the same. So if you see a word in the text that is the same as a word in the question, it is not automatically the correct answer.

Example:

I played a lot of sports after school when I was younger.

This is **NOT** the correct answer to the example question because the meaning is different from the question.

Reading Practice: Multiple Matching

1 <u>Underline</u> the most important words in these questions.

1 Which person does <u>a lot of sports</u> on the <u>weekend</u>?

Which person …

2 loves trying new activities after school?

3 has a lot of online friends?

4 reads science and nature magazines on the Internet?

5 wants to study art or drama at school next year?

6 doesn't have any aunts, uncles, or cousins?

7 doesn't like living in a big city?

Tip!
Underlining the most important words in the questions helps you to remember the information you need to find in the text.

2 Match words 1–10 with their opposites in the box.

> after   boring   difficult   evening   finish   good   hate   late   short   ~~small~~

1 big ___small___

2 easy _____   5 long _____   8 morning _____

3 early _____   6 start _____   9 fun _____

4 love _____   7 before _____   10 bad _____

Tip!
When reading the text, look for words or phrases that are opposites (often with a negative verb), or synonyms of the words in the question.

3 Read the text and match the words in **bold** with the synonyms (1–9).

One place on my **road** that's very popular with **young people** is the skate park. Some of my friends spend all their free time there. There is also a **big** gym near me, with some **good** **courses**, like swimming and dancing. **Many** of my friends **tell me** they would like to go there, too, but the **price** is too high. I **travel** to a cheaper gym, but it's not very near my house and so it's **difficult** to get to.

1 street ___road___   3 large _____   5 teenagers _____   7 go _____   9 classes _____

2 a lot _____   4 say _____   6 hard _____   8 cost _____

4 Choose the option, A or B, that has the same meaning as the question.

0 Which person has a lot of homework to do?

(A) I spend about two hours every night on school work.

B In my school, the teachers don't usually give us much homework.

1 Which person isn't happy about their hair color?

A I have red hair, but I don't mind. It's the same as Ed Sheeran's!

B Everyone in my family has blond hair. It's boring. I want to be different.

2 Which person reads information about science on the Internet?

A There is so much interesting stuff to read online these days, especially science articles.

B I love reading my dad's science magazines. He buys them every month.

3 Which person doesn't mind getting up early in the morning?

A I have to get up at seven so I'm not late for school, but that isn't a problem.

B I'm glad when it's Saturday and I can get up late.

4 Which person thinks living in the country is boring?

A People say that the country is boring, but I think there's a lot to do.

B I'm happy I live in the city. I'm sure it's more exciting than being in a small town.

EXAM TIPS: Writing Skills

Writing: A Short Email or Note

You will write a short email or note of 25 words or more. The instructions in the test tell you exactly what you need to do.

Example:

*You want to **go to the movies** with **your friend** Jan on **Saturday**. Write an email to Jan.*

The instructions also explain three things you need to include in the text. For example:

In the email:

- **ask** Jan to **go to the movies** with you
- say **what movie** you want to see
- say **where** you can **meet**.

Exam Guide: Writing a Short Email or Note

- Read the instructions carefully and decide what kind of message is required.
- It is important to include all the points from the instructions in the text. It is also better to keep them in the same order as in the instructions.
- The text needs
  - an opening sentence
  - three sentences, one for each point
  - a sentence to close (for example a question asking your friend's opinion)
  - (in an email) your name at the end.
- When you finish, read the text again and count the number of words. If you have included all the information from the plan above, the text should be at least 25 words. If it's more, that's OK. If you haven't written 25 words, go back and check that you have included all the points and the opening and the closing sentences.

Writing: A Short Story

You will write a short story of 35 words or more. To help you there are three pictures. You write the story they show.

Exam Guide: Writing a Short Story

- Don't start writing immediately. Look at the pictures for a minute and decide what the story is about. A good way to plan a story is to think about *Who? Where? When?* and *What?*
- Give any people in the picture a name. Then write any useful vocabulary you want to use (nouns, verbs, adjectives, etc.) next to each picture.
- Decide how to start (e.g., *One day/Yesterday*). Use the past tense when you write your story.
- When you finish writing, count the words. You need to write at least 35 words.

REMEMBER!
You will receive a piece of paper to write notes or a draft. Use it to plan your writing.

Writing Practice: An Email or Note; a Short Story

1 Match the phrases from a text message with the right category A–C.

Tip! Try to use different phrases for inviting and suggesting ideas.

> A opening   B inviting or suggesting   C closing phrase

1 I'd like to see the new X-Men movie. __B__

2 What do you think? _____

3 Do you want to go swimming this afternoon? _____

4 Let me know soon. _____

5 Hey _____

6 Can we meet at the bus stop at seven? _____

7 Hi, Jan _____

8 We can try the new pool. _____

9 How about going to the movies on Saturday? _____

2 Order the words to make sentences from an email.

1 cheap / to / a / go / restaurant / Let's / .   Let's go to a cheap restaurant.

2 want / during / Do / break / to / you / meet / the / ?

5 Tania / Hi / ,

3 for / Why / days / we / don't / go / a few / camping / ?

6 climbing / I'd / go / again / to / like / .

4 what / know / Let / you / me / think / .

7 my / can / tent / take / We / brother's / .

3 Separate the text into words and sentences. Then rewrite the email with the correct format and punctuation in your notebook.

Tip! Always check your writing for spelling or punctuation.

heyjosedoyouwanttohangouttogetheronsaturdaywecangotothe
newshoppingmallcanlicometoyourhouseatfourletmeknowsooncarlos

Hey José,

4 Correct the spelling of these words.

1 swiming   ___swimming___

2 shoping   _____

3 wich   _____

4 tenis   _____

5 Wenesday   _____

6 tomorow   _____

7 bycicle   _____

8 diferent   _____

9 scool   _____

10 begining   _____

5 Put the words in the box in the correct place in the story.

Tip! Use time words like *yesterday*, *after*, and *then* to make the order of events clear. Use words like *but* and *so* to show how the events connect.

> After   but   so   Then   ~~Yesterday~~

0 __Yesterday__ Annie had a technology presentation at school, 1_____ she got up late. 2_____ she got to school, she saw her notes weren't in her bag. They were important, 3_____ she called her dad and asked him to look for them. He found them in her room. 4_____ he brought her notes to school. She was very happy.

EXAM TIPS: Listening Skills

Listening: Three-Option Multiple Choice

You will listen to five short texts. You will hear the text twice. Each text is about something different, and the question usually explains who is speaking, who they are speaking to, and what they are talking about.

Example:

*You will hear **two friends** talking about **their plans for the weekend**.*

You then have to answer a question about each text, with three options, A, B, and C.

Example:

*You will hear two friends talking about their plans for the weekend. **What do they both plan to do?***

*A They are **both going** to a **basketball game**.*

*B They are **both visiting** their **grandparents**.*

*C They are **both going shopping** with **friends**.*

You can write your answers on the question paper.

Exam Guide: Three-Option Multiple Choice

- Read the questions before you listen. Read the questions carefully because they tell you what to listen for.

- <u>Underline</u> the important words in the question. In the example, the most important word in the question is **both**.
  Example:
  What do they <u>both</u> plan to do?
  A They are both going to a <u>basketball game</u>.
  B They are both visiting their <u>grandparents</u>.
  C They are both going <u>shopping</u> with <u>friends</u>.

- When you listen the first time, try to decide what the correct answer is and circle A, B, or C. If you're not sure, don't worry. The second time you listen, you can check your first answer or decide for the first time.

- Sometimes the first time you listen, you hear that one answer is definitely wrong. Cross it out. Then the second time you listen, just focus on the other two possible answers.

- Always give an answer, even if you don't know which one is correct. You don't lose points for a wrong answer.

- When you have heard one text twice, don't spend a lot of time thinking about it. Focus on the next listening text when it starts.

REMEMBER!

You will usually hear the people talk about all the possible answers in some way, but this is a "trap." Only one answer is correct.

To avoid traps, listen carefully to every word. You will hear negative verbs (for example: *I'm not visiting my grandparents this weekend*) or things which are similar but not the same as the correct answer (for example: *I'm going shopping with my sister on Saturday*).

Listening Practice: Three-Option Multiple Choice

🎧 **1** Listen to the sentences. Mark (✓) if they are affirmative or (✗) if they are negative.
E.01

1 _____ 2 _____ 3 _____ 4 _____ 5 _____ 6 _____

🎧 **2** Is the meaning of the sentences you hear the same as sentences 1–6? Write *Y* (yes) or *N* (no).
E.02

1 I decided not to buy the shirt because I didn't like the color. _____

2 It takes Martin a quarter of an hour to walk home. _____

3 It was sunny yesterday. _____

4 Martin is flying to Spain on vacation. _____

5 Paula's sister has dark hair. _____

6 The teacher tells Eric to do his homework again. _____

🎧 **3** Read sentences 1–6. Then listen and correct the information that is different.
E.03

1 Alex went to Scotland by bus last year. _____

2 Laia is going to stay in a hotel with her grandparents. _____

3 Donna usually goes to the bowling alley on the weekend. _____

4 Harry's mom lost her bus pass yesterday. _____

5 Last week, Megan saw a show about bears on TV. _____

6 Tom has a basketball game on Saturday morning. _____

🎧 **4** Listen and choose the correct option, A or B. You will hear each text twice.
E.04

1 The teacher has a problem with Sarah's homework because …

  A she made a lot of mistakes.

  B she did the wrong page.

2 What's the weather like today?

  A It's cold and wet.

  B It's cloudy and warm.

3 What did Corrin and Vanessa do today?

  A They went out for a meal.

  B They went out with school friends.

4 How did Nico get home after the concert?

  A He caught the last bus.

  B His friend's dad gave him a ride.

5 What did Ollie buy at the shopping mall?

  A a new gym bag

  B some new sweatpants

6 What does Chloe's mother want her to do?

  A go shopping

  B clean her room

Subject Pronouns

Singul	Plural
I	we
you	you
he / she / it	they

- We use a subject pronoun before a verb.
  She is Brazilian. (NOT *Is Brazilian.*)
- The singular and plural form of **you** is the same.

Possessive Adjectives

Singular	Plural
my	our
your	your
his / her / its	their

- We use possessive adjectives to show that something belongs to somebody. We always use possessive adjectives with a noun.
  Our house is big.   Their school is fun.

Verb *To Be*

Affirmative	Negative
I'm Mexican.	I'm not Mexican.
You're Mexican.	You aren't Mexican.
He's / She's / It's Mexican.	He / She / It isn't Mexican.
We're Mexican.	We aren't Mexican.
You're Mexican.	You aren't Mexican.
They're Mexican.	They aren't Mexican.

Questions	Short Answers	
	Affirmative	Negative
Am I Mexican?	Yes, I am.	No, I'm not.
Are you Mexican?	Yes, you are.	No, you aren't.
Is he / she / it Mexican?	Yes, he / she / it is.	No, he / she / it isn't.
Are we Mexican?	Yes, we are.	No we aren't.
Are you Mexican?	Yes, you are.	No, you aren't.
Are they Mexican?	Yes, they are.	No, they aren't.

- We use **verb to be** to identify or describe something.
  They're red.   He's Spanish.   It's good.
- We usually use contractions in conversation.
  We're from Canada.   She's ten.

- We change the word order in questions; we put **to be** before the subject.
  Is David OK?   Are you from London?
  (NOT *You are from London?*)
- We usually reply with short answers.
  A: *Is it blue?* **B:** *Yes, it is.*   **A:** *Is it red?* **B:** *No, it isn't.*

Question Words

- We use **what** to ask for information.
  What is your favorite color?
- We use **where** to ask about places.
  Where are you from?
- We use **when** to ask about time.
  When is your birthday?
- We use **how old** to ask about age.
  How old is your father?
- We use **who** to ask about people.
  Who is your best friend?

Whose + Possessive Pronouns

Whose book is this?	Singular	Plural
	It's mine.	It's ours.
	It's yours.	It's yours.
	It's his / hers.	It's theirs.

- **Whose** asks about possession or ownership.
- We often use possessive pronouns to answer **whose** questions. They help us to avoid repeating information.
  Whose pencil is this? It's mine. (instead of *It's my pencil.*)
  We don't use **its** as a possessive pronoun.
  Whose book is this? (NOT *It's its.*)
- We use **this** (singular) and **these** (plural) to talk about things that are near.
  This is my pencil.   These are my books.
- We use **that** (singular) and **those** (plural) to talk about things that are not near.
  That is my bag.   Those are my pens.

Imperatives

Affirmative	Negative
Stand up!	Don't stand up!
Open the book!	Don't open the book!

- We use the imperative to give orders or instructions.
  Come here, please.
- We use **don't** to form the negative.
  Don't write in your textbook.

GRAMMAR PRACTICE

Subject Pronouns and Possessive Adjectives

1 Complete the sentences with the correct subject pronouns and possessive adjectives.

1 My best friend Maria is from Paris. ___She___ 's French. ___Her___ house is very big!

2 My name's Pablo. _____ 'm from Ecuador. I'm in _____ classroom.

3 Berat and Ahmet are Turkish. _____ 're from Istanbul. These are _____ books.

4 My English teacher is Mr. Jones. _____ 's from New York. _____ classes are fun!

5 Susie, _____ 're my friend! Today is _____ birthday! Happy birthday!

Verb *To Be*

2 (Circle) the correct form of the verb *to be*.

Hi, my name ¹(*is*)/ *are* Alicia. My favorite color ²*is* / *are* blue. I ³*are* / *am* 12 years old. My best friends ⁴*is* / *are* Laura and Eva. They ⁵*isn't* / *aren't* from Mexico like me. They are from China. We ⁶*is* / *are* in school today.

3 Match questions 1–6 with answers a–f.

1 Are you hungry? [d]
2 Is your school big? [ ]
3 Is he in the room? [ ]
4 Is she from China? [ ]
5 Are we 12 years old? [ ]
6 Are they Canadian? [ ]

a Yes, we are.
b No, she isn't.
c No, it isn't.
d ~~Yes, I am!~~
e No, they aren't.
f Yes, he is.

Question Words

4 Complete the conversation with the words in the box.

| How old   When   ~~Where~~   Who |

A: Hi, Mateo. ¹ ___Where___ are you from?
B: I'm from Argentina.
A: ² _____ are you?
B: I'm 13.
A: ³ _____ 's your birthday?
B: It's in February.
A: ⁴ _____ 's your favorite singer?
B: Taylor Swift. She's great!

Whose + Possessive Pronouns

5 Write the words in the correct order to make questions. Then complete the answers with the correct possessive pronouns.

1 book / is / Whose / this /?
___Whose book is this?___
It's my book. It's ___mine.___ .

2 is / this / Whose / dictionary / ?
_____
It's your dictionary. It's _____ .

3 calculator / is / Whose / that / ?
_____
It's his calculator. It's _____ .

4 these / pens / Whose / are / ?
_____
They're her pens. They're _____ .

5 notebooks / those / are / Whose / ?
_____
They're our notebooks. They're _____ .

6 desks / are / Whose / those / ?
_____
They're their desks. They're _____ .

Imperatives

6 Write the affirmative or the negative.

1 Write on the paper.
___Don't write on the paper.___

2 _____
Don't use your calculator.

3 Use your dictionary.
_____

4 _____
Don't listen to your teacher.

5 Close the door.
_____

6 _____
Don't do your homework.

GRAMMAR REFERENCE

To Have: Affirmative and Negative

Affirmative		Negative	
I have		I don't have	
You have		You don't have	
He / She / It has	short hair.	He / She / It doesn't have	brown eyes.
We have		We don't have	
You have		You don't have	
They have		They don't have	

- We use **have** to talk about possession.
  I have five cousins.   *She has 12 grandchildren.*

- To make the negative, we put **don't / doesn't** before **have**.
  We don't have a big house.
  She doesn't have a sister.

Possessive 's

Singular Nouns	Plural Nouns	Irregular Plural Nouns
Beth's computer	His parents' house	The women's soccer team
Carlos's bike	The students' books	The children's favorite toy

- We use **apostrophe + s** to indicate possession.
  This is Andrea's notebook.

- We put **'s** after a singular name or noun and **s'** after a plural name or noun.
  Carla's phone (NOT *The phone of Carla*)
  His grandparents' house (NOT *The house of his grandparents*)

- Some plural nouns are irregular. To show possession, we add **'s**.
  men's, people's, children's

- When two people possess something, we use **'s** after the second noun.
  Paul and Amy's family
  Mom and Dad's computer

To Have: Questions

	Question	Short Answers	
		Affirmative	**Negative**
Do	I have a blue book?	Yes, I do.	No, I don't.
	you have a blue book?	Yes, you do.	No, you don't.
	we have a blue book?	Yes, we do.	No, we don't.
	you have a blue book?	Yes, you do.	No, you don't.
	they have a blue book?	Yes, they do.	No, they don't.
Does	he / she / it have a blue book?	Yes, he / she / it does.	No, he / she / it doesn't.

- We use **do** + **subject** + **have** + **object** in questions.
  Do you have a bike?   Does your mom have a cousin?

- In spoken English, we reply to questions with short answers.
  A: Do you have a brother?
  B: Yes, I do. (NOT Yes, I do have.) / No, I don't. (NOT No, I don't have.)

How Many ... Do You Have?

- We use **how many** + **object** + **do** + **subject** + **have** in questions to ask about the number of things.
  A: How many cousins does he have?   B: He has 30.
  A: How many brothers and sisters do you have?   B: I have two sisters. I don't have a brother.

GRAMMAR PRACTICE

To Have: Affirmative and Negative

1 Complete the sentences with the correct affirmative form of *to have*.

1 I _____have_____ a dictionary.

2 We _____ six red pens.

3 My aunt _____ three sisters.

4 Mom and Dad _____ a mobile home.

5 You _____ 12 cousins.

6 Our house _____ five bedrooms.

2 Write the sentences in the negative.

1 I have two brothers.
I don't have two brothers.

2 We have a new teacher at school.
_____

3 My grandma has ten grandchildren.
_____

4 My best friends have green uniforms.
_____

5 He has a bike.
_____

6 We have a big house.
_____

3 Look at the chart and complete the text with the correct form of *to have*.

	Javier	Rosa
sisters	1	2
brothers	0	1
cousins	2	2
bike	1	0
computer	0	0

Javier [1] _has_ one sister; her name is Cecilia. He [2] _____ any brothers. He [3] _____ a blue bike. Rosa [4] _____ two sisters and one brother. She [5] _____ a bike. Javier and Rosa [6] _____ two cousins. They [7] _____ a computer.

Possessive *'s*

4 Write *s'* or *'s* in the correct places in the sentences.

1 My ~~dad~~ bike is gray and my ~~uncle~~ bike is black.
___dad's___ and my uncle's _____

2 Natalia favorite color is green and her sister is blue.
_____

3 His grandparent house is big, but his parent house is small.
_____

4 Myra family are from India, and Diego family are from Spain.
_____

5 Vero and Isaac English books are red. Their mom book is yellow.
_____

To Have: Questions

5 Write the words in the correct order to make questions. Then match them with answers a–e.

1 have / I / Do / book / an / English / ?
Do I have an English book? ___d___

2 bike / a / Do / blue / have / you / ?
_____

3 pets / Alex / Does / two / have / ?
_____

4 Catalina / brother / have / a / Does / ?
_____

5 big / have / house / Do / they / a / ?
_____

a Yes, he does. He has two cats.   ~~d Yes, you do.~~

b No, she doesn't. She has a sister.   e No, I don't. It's green.

c Yes, they do.

How Many ... Do You Have?

6 Write questions with *How many* for the answers.

1 _How many cousins do you have?_
I have three cousins.

2 _____
My mom has two nephews.

3 _____
We have 20 teachers at our school.

4 _____
My best friend has two sisters.

5 _____
We have four subjects on Friday.

Simple Present: Affirmative and Negative

Affirmative	
I live	
You live	in Lima.
He / She / It lives	
We / You / They live	
Negative	
I don't live	
You don't live	in Lima.
He / She / It doesn't live	
We / You / They don't live	

- We use the simple present to talk about facts, habits, and routines.
  I speak Chinese.   He goes to school. They study English.
- We form the negative of the simple present with the **subject** + ***don't*** / ***doesn't*** + **infinitive**.
  They don't speak English.
- We use ***doesn't*** in the third person (*he / she / it*).
  He doesn't do his homework.

Spelling: Third Person

- The third person form (*he / she / it*) of the simple present ends in **-s**.
  eat – he eats   read – she reads
- With verbs ending in **consonant** + ***y***, we replace the ***y*** with ***-ies*** for the *he / she / it* forms.
  study – she studies
- The *he / she / it* form of verbs ending in ***-ss***, ***-sh***, ***-ch***, ***-x***, and ***-o*** is ***-es***.
  *kiss – she kisses   relax – he relaxes
  finish – he finishes   go – she goes
  teach – she teaches*
- Some verbs have an irregular spelling in the third person.
  have – she has   be – he is

Adverbs of Frequency

never   sometimes   often   usually   always

0% $\longleftarrow$ $\longrightarrow$ 100%

- Adverbs of frequency say how often we do something. They go after the verb *to be* but before all other verbs.
  She's always happy.   He sometimes checks his phone in the afternoons. We usually do homework after school.
- With ***never***, we always use an affirmative verb.
  I never go out with my friends on Monday.
- In questions, adverbs of frequency always come after the subject.
  Do you always have English class on Wednesday?

Simple Present: Questions

Questions		Short Answers	
		Affirmative	**Negative**
Do	I like oranges?	Yes, I do.	No, I don't.
	you like oranges?	Yes, you do.	No, you don't.
Does	he / she / it like oranges?	Yes, he / she / it does.	No, he / she / it doesn't.
Do	we like oranges?	Yes, we do.	No, we don't.
	you like oranges?	Yes, you do.	No, you don't.
	they like oranges?	Yes, they do.	No, they don't.

- We form simple present ***Yes/No*** questions with ***do/does*** + **subject** + **infinitive**.
  Do you brush your teeth in the morning? Does she go to bed at 9 p.m.?
- We use short answers with ***do/does***. We don't repeat the main verb.
  *A: Do you often go to school by car? B: Yes, I do.
  A: Does he live in London?   B: No, he doesn't.*

Wh- Questions

Question Word	*Do/Does*	Subject	Verb
Who	do	you	live (with)?
What time	does	the party	start?
Where	does	she	live?
What	does	his dad	do?
When	do	they	play?

- We form ***Wh-*** questions with a **question word** + ***do/does*** + **subject** + **verb**.
  What time do you go to bed? (NOT ~~What time you go to bed~~?)
  Where does he go to school?
- We also use the question ***How often ... ?*** to ask about frequency.
  How often do you play video games?

GRAMMAR PRACTICE

Simple Present: Affirmative and Negative

1 Write the words in the correct order to make sentences.

1 I / every / day / wake / up / at / 7 p.m.
   I wake up at 7 p.m. every day.

2 gets / up / takes / a / Antonio / shower / when / he
   _____

3 have / homework / Isa / Mondays / doesn't / on
   _____

4 don't / brothers / My / at / 8:30 p.m. / to / bed / go
   _____

5 lunch / school / We / have / at
   _____

6 my / with / homework / helps / My / dad / me
   _____

2 Complete the text with the simple present form of the verbs in parentheses.

On Saturday mornings, Chloe [1] _gets up_ (get up) at 9 a.m. She [2] _____ (take) a shower and [3] _____ (brush) her teeth. Then she [4] _____ (get dressed) and [5] _____ (have) her favorite breakfast: toast and fruit juice. She [6] _____ (not see) her dad on Saturday mornings because he [7] _____ (go) to work.

At 10 a.m., she [8] _____ (go) to see her best friends, Grace and Ella. They [9] _____ (not live) near Chloe. She [10] _____ (go) on the bus to see them. Chloe [11] _____ (stay) at their house for about two hours. Then she [12] _____ (get) the bus to her grandma's house. She [13] _____ (visit) her grandma on Saturdays because she [14] _____ (not see) her during the week.

Adverbs of Frequency

3 Circle the correct options.

1 I _____ early in the morning.
   a usually get up   **b** get up usually

2 I _____ sports on the weekend.
   a play often   **b** often play

3 I _____ lunch with my sister at school.
   a sometimes have   **b** have sometimes

4 I _____ my homework in the evening.
   a do always   **b** always do

5 I _____ burgers for dinner.
   a never eat   **b** eat never

Simple Present: Questions

4 Complete the questions and answers. Use the verbs in parentheses.

1 _Do_ you _play_ tennis on the weekend? (play)
   No, I _don't_ .

2 _____ your cousin _____ to your school? (go)
   Yes, he _____ ! He's in my class.

3 _____ your parents _____ Spanish? (speak)
   No, they _____ .

4 _____ you often _____ your phone? (check)
   Yes, I _____ .

5 _____ your aunt _____ in the United States? (live)
   No, she _____ .

6 _____ your sister _____ her school uniform? (like)
   Yes, she _____ .

Wh- Questions

5 Complete the questions with the words in the box.

How often	What	What time	~~When~~	Where	Who

1 _When_ do you go to school?
2 _____ do your aunt and uncle live?
3 _____ does your dad do?
4 _____ do you walk to school with?
5 _____ do you have exams at school?
6 _____ does your mom get up?

6 Match the answers (a–f) with the questions in Exercise 5.

a My best friend.   _4_
b From Monday to Friday.   ____
c In front of my house!   ____
d Every month!   ____
e He's an English teacher!   ____
f At seven o'clock during the week
  and eight o'clock on the weekend.   ____

Can for Ability and Permission

Affirmative			Negative	
I			I	
You			You	
He / She / It	can play		He / She / It	can't play
We	the piano.		We	the piano.
You			You	
They			They	

- We use **can** to express ability or permission.
  He can play the guitar. (ability)
  Dad says we can play video games tonight. (permission)
- **Can** is the same in all forms. The *he/she/it* form doesn't end in **-s**.
  She can speak Portuguese.
- We always use the infinitive without **to** after **can**.
  They can go to school.
  (NOT *They can to go to school.*)

Can: Questions

| Yes/No Questions | Short Answers | |
	Affirmative	Negative
Can I go?	Yes, I can.	No, I can't.
Can you go?	Yes, you can.	No, you can't.
Can he / she / it go?	Yes, he / she / it can.	No, he / she / it can't.
Can we go?	Yes, we can.	No, we can't.
Can you go?	Yes, you can.	No, you can't.
Can they go?	Yes, they can.	No, they can't.

- We change the word order when we form questions. We don't use **do/does**.
  Can you use your dictionary at school?
  (NOT *Do you can use your dictionary at school?*)
- We use the adverbs **very well**, **well**, **quite well**, **not very well**, **badly**, or **not at all** to describe how we are able to do things.
  A: Can you play the guitar?   *B: Yes, but not very well.*

Verb Forms: (*Don't*) *Like, Don't Mind, Love, Hate + -ing*

- We use the **-ing** form of the verb after **like**, **don't like**, **don't mind**, **love**, and **hate**.
  She loves reading books. (NOT *She loves read books.*)
  I don't mind going to school. (NOT *I don't mind go to school.*)
- We can also use nouns after these verbs.
  They don't mind geography, but they love history.

Object Pronouns

Subject Pronoun	I	you	he	she	it	we	you	they
Object Pronoun	me	you	him	her	it	us	you	them

- We use object pronouns after some verbs and prepositions.
  She meets <u>my sister and me</u> after school every day. – She meets <u>us</u> after school every day.
  I usually have lunch with <u>my friends</u>. – I usually have lunch with <u>them</u>.
- For animals and things, we use **it** (singular) and **them** (plural).
  Don't feed the bird! – Don't feed it!
  Do you read books? – Do you read them?
- We can also put an object pronoun after **like**, **don't like**, **don't mind**, **love**, and **hate**.
  This is my new book. Do you like it? (NOT *Do you like?*)
  I don't like Mondays. I hate them.

GRAMMAR PRACTICE

Can for Ability and Permission

1 Write sentences with *can*. Then write *A* (ability) or *P* (permission).

1 Daniel / sing / very well
   Daniel can sing very well.   A

2 My dad / speak / French
   _____

3 I / use / my dad's / computer / in the evening
   _____

4 My brother / dance / well
   _____

5 Harry / play / the guitar well
   _____

6 You / use my / phone
   _____

2 Change the sentences in Exercise 1 to the negative.

1 *Daniel can't sing very well.*
2 _____
3 _____
4 _____
5 _____
6 _____

Can: Questions

3 Look at the chart and write questions and answers about Alberto and Sara.

	Alberto	Sara
take good photos	✔	✘
paint well	✘	✔
dance salsa	✔	✘

1 *Can Alberto take good photos?*   Yes, he can.
2 _____
3 _____
4 _____
5 _____
6 _____

Verb Forms: (*Don't*) *Like, Don't Mind, Love, Hate + -ing*

4 Complete the text with the words in parentheses.

My sister [1] __loves going__ (love / go) to school.
She [2] _____ (like / study). I'm different!
I [3] _____ (love / see) my friends at school.
I [4] _____ (not mind / learn) new things,
but I [5] _____ (not like / take) exams and
I [6] _____ (hate / get up) early every day!

Object Pronouns

5 Match questions 1–5 with answers a–e. Then circle the correct object pronouns.

1 Do you like listening to your teacher?   b
2 Does your brother talk a lot? _____
3 Do you love hanging out with your friends? _____
4 Can your friends help you and your sister? _____
5 Do you always go to judo classes? _____

a Yes, he does, but I don't listen to *it / him*.
b Yes, I love listening to *me /* (*her*).
c Yes, and my cousin comes to classes with *him / me*.
d Yes, I do. I meet *them / it* every day.
e No, they can't help *us / you*.

6 Rewrite the sentences with the object pronouns in the box.

her   him   it   them   ~~them~~   us

1 I like hanging out with my friends.
   I like hanging out with them.

2 I can't find my pen.
   _____

3 I like my aunt.
   _____

4 They can't see you or me.
   _____

5 I love chatting online with my cousin, David!
   _____

6 I visit my grandparents on Sundays.
   _____

Countable and Uncountable Nouns

- Countable nouns can be counted individually. They have a singular and a plural form.
  one apple – two apples   *one book – three books*
- Uncountable nouns can't be counted individually. They don't have a plural and are always singular.
  bread (NOT ~~a bread~~)   *milk* (NOT ~~a milk~~)   *homework* (NOT ~~a homework~~)   *music* (NOT ~~a music~~)

A/An, Some/Any

	Singular Countable	Plural Countable	Uncountable
Affirmative	I have an orange.	I have some tomatoes.	I have some chocolate.
Negative	I don't have an orange.	I don't have any tomatoes.	I don't have any chocolate.
Question	Do you have an orange?	Do you have any tomatoes?	Do you have any chocolate?

- We use **a** with singular countable nouns.
  a banana   a cat   a snack
- We use **an** with singular countable nouns when the noun starts with a vowel sound.
  an orange   an uncle

- We use **some** and **any** when we don't know a quantity or it's not important.
- We use **some** and **any** with plural countable nouns. **Some** is usually used in affirmative sentences and **any** in negative sentences and questions.
  We need some apples.   He doesn't have any tomatoes.   Do we have any carrots?
- We also use **some** and **any** with uncountable nouns. **Some** is usually used in affirmative sentences, and **any** in negative sentences and questions.
  We need some juice.   Marta doesn't have any water.   Do we have any rice?

There Is/Isn't, There Are/Aren't

	Singular	Plural
Affirmative	There's a quiz today.	There are some eggs on the table.
Negative	There isn't a quiz today.	There aren't any eggs on the table.
Questions	Is there a quiz today?	Are there any eggs on the table?
Short Answers	Yes, there is. No, there isn't.	Yes, there are. No, there aren't.

- We use **there is** with singular countable and uncountable nouns.
  There is a school.
  There is some cheese. (NOT *There ~~are~~ some cheese.*)
- We use **there are** with plural countable nouns.
  There are some potatoes.   There are four pizzas.
- In questions and negatives we usually use **any** with plural countable and uncountable nouns.
  Are there any bananas?   Is there any milk?
  There aren't any burgers.   There isn't any bread.
- In informal English we can use the contraction **there's**, but we don't use a contraction for **there are**.

Much/Many, A Lot Of

	Countable Plural	Uncountable
Affirmative	There are a lot of eggs.	There's a lot of cheese.
Negative	There aren't many eggs.	There isn't much cheese.
Questions	How many eggs are there?	How much cheese is there?

- We use **much**, **many**, and **a lot of** to express quantity.
- We use **much** in negative sentences with uncountable nouns.
  There isn't much water.
- We use **many** in negative sentences with countable nouns.
  There aren't many tomatoes.
- We use **a lot of** in affirmative sentences with plural countable and uncountable nouns to describe a big quantity of something.
  There are a lot of vegetables.   We have a lot of rice.
- We use **how many** with plural countable nouns and **how much** with uncountable nouns to ask about quantity.
  How many carrots are there?   How much juice do you have?

GRAMMAR PRACTICE

Countable and Uncountable Nouns

1 (Circle) the correct options.

1 I have an (apple) / *oranges* in my bag.
2 Alba has some *potato* / *meat* for lunch.
3 I have a *banana* / *bread*.
4 He doesn't have an *cheese* / *egg* for breakfast.
5 We don't have any *chocolate* / *carrot*.
6 They have some *pear* / *milk*.

A/An, Some/Any

2 Complete the sentences with *a*, *an*, *some*, or *any*.

1 We need __some__ milk and __some__ eggs.
2 I have _____ apple and _____ cheese for lunch.
3 Do you have _____ oranges, Mom? I want to make _____ orange juice.
4 We can't make a cake! We don't have _____ eggs!
5 I want to make a sandwich. I need _____ tomato and _____ egg.
6 Let's buy _____ bottle of soda and _____ fruit at the supermarket.

There Is/Isn't, There Are/Aren't

3 Complete the conversation with the correct form of *there is* / *there are*.

A: Let's make a salad!
B: [1] __Are there__ any tomatoes?
A: Yes, [2]_____ , but [3]_____ any onions.
B: OK, that's not a problem. [4]_____ some cheese, and [5]_____ ten carrots.
A: I don't want ten carrots in my salad! Let's make spaghetti!
B: Sorry! [6]_____ any pasta!

4 Write sentences about the food and drink words in the box. Use the correct form of *there is* / *there are* and *some* or *any*.

> apples ✔ bread ✗ carrots ✔ eggs ✗ water ✔ bananas ✗

1 _There are some apples._
2 _____
3 _____
4 _____
5 _____
6 _____

Much/Many, A Lot Of

5 (Circle) the correct options. Then match questions 1–5 with answers a–f.

1 How (much) / *many* fruit do you eat every day? [e]
2 How *much* / *many* people are there in your family? ☐
3 Do you spend *much* / *many* time checking your phone? ☐
4 How *many* / *much* snacks do you have every day? ☐
5 How *much* / *many* water do you drink at home? ☐
6 Are there *much* / *many* bottles of soda in your fridge? ☐

a There are seven: I have a lot of brothers and sisters!
b About two liters a day – more if I play tennis.
c There aren't any. We only drink water and milk at home.
d No! I don't have much time to look at it!
e I eat an apple every morning.
f I don't eat any! I'm too busy.

Present Continuous: Affirmative and Negative

Affirmative		Negative	
I'm		I'm not	
You're		You're not	
He's / She's / It's	eating dinner.	He's / She's / It's not	eating dinner.
We're		We're not	
You're		You're not	
They're		They're not	

- We use the present continuous to talk about actions in progress at the time of speaking.
  You are reading this sentence.
- For the affirmative, we use **subject** + **to be** + **verb** + **-ing**.
  The dog is sleeping.   The children are playing.
- For the negative, we put **not** after **to be**.
  She is not (isn't) downloading songs.

Present Continuous: Questions

(Question Word)	To Be	Subject	Verb + -ing
-	Am	I	reading?
-	Are	you	thinking?
-	Is	he / she / it	sleeping?
-	Are	we / you / they	learning?
What	are	you	doing?
Where	is	she	going?

Short Answers	
Affirmative	**Negative**
Yes, I am.	No, I'm not.
Yes, you are.	No, you aren't.
Yes, he / she / it is.	No, he / she / it isn't.
Yes, we / you / they are.	No, we / you / they aren't.

- To form questions, we use **to be** + **subject** + **verb** + **-ing**.
  Are you listening?
- We don't use the **verb** + **-ing** in short answers.
  Yes, I am. (NOT Yes, I am listening.)
- We form information questions with the **Wh-** question word before *be*.
  Who are you talking to?   What are they doing?

Spelling: -ing Form

- With most verbs, we add **-ing** to the infinitive.
  eat – eating   read – reading   think – thinking
- For verbs ending in **-e**, we remove the **-e** and add **-ing**.
  write – writing   have – having   give – giving
- For verbs ending in a vowel and a consonant, we double the final consonant and add **-ing**.
  *stop – stopping   shop – shopping
  plan – planning*

Simple Present and Present Continuous

- We use the simple present to talk about facts, habits, and routines.
  *Red and yellow make orange.
  I read a lot of books.
  He usually wears boots.*
- We use the present continuous to talk about actions in progress at the time of speaking.
  *I read a lot of books. At the moment, I'm reading a really good one.
  He usually wears boots, but he's wearing sneakers today.*
- Some verbs are not usually used in the continuous form: **hate**, **know**, **like**, **love**, **need**, **remember**, **think**, **understand**, **want**.
  I like that song. (NOT I'm liking that song.)
- We use expressions like **at the moment** and **right now** with the present continuous.
  He's playing video games at the moment.

GRAMMAR PRACTICE

Present Continuous: Affirmative and Negative

1 Write the *-ing* form of the verbs.

1 eat   *eating*
2 write
3 chat
4 play
5 swim
6 have

2 Complete the sentences with the present continuous form of the verbs in the box.

> chat   get dressed   have   listen   ~~read~~   use

1 Luis   *is reading*   a book.
2 My grandparents _____ their dinner.
3 The teacher _____ to our stories.
4 My mom _____ to go to a party this evening.
5 You _____ my computer in school today.
6 I _____ with my friends online.

3 Rewrite the sentences in Exercise 2 in the negative form of the present continuous. Use contractions.

1 *Luis isn't reading a book.*
2
3
4
5
6

Present Continuous: Questions

4 Complete the questions with the present continuous form of the verbs in parentheses. Then write the short answers.

1 ___*Are*___ you ___*doing*___ (do) your homework?
Yes, ___*I am*___.
2 _____ your sister _____ (read) a book?
No, _____.
3 _____ your uncle _____ (make) dinner?
Yes, _____.
4 _____ we _____ (have) sandwiches for lunch?
No, _____.
5 _____ my grandparents _____ (watch) TV?
No, _____.
6 _____ the cat _____ (sleep) on my bed?
Yes, _____.

Simple Present and Present Continuous

5 Complete the rules. Write *present continuous* or *simple present*.

1 To talk about facts, routines, and habits, we use the _____.
2 To talk about an action in progress at the time of speaking, we use the _____.
3 We use *always, often, usually, sometimes,* and *never* with the _____.
4 We use *right now* and *at the moment* with the _____.

6 (Circle) the correct options.

My name is Carolina. At the moment, I'm on vacation and I [1]*help* / (*'m helping*) my dad. We have a big yard, and he usually [2]*works* / *is working* all the time, so he's tired on the weekend. Now he is on vacation, too. I [3]*like* / *'m liking* flowers, and we usually [4]*collect* / *are collecting* some to put in the house. Right now, my dad [5]*paints* / *is painting* the fence and, of course, my brother [6]*watches* / *is watching* us do all the work!

Comparatives

Comparatives	
Short Adjectives smart	add -**er**: smarter
Short Adjectives Ending in Vowel + Consonant big	double the final consonant and add -**er**: bigger
Adjectives Ending in -e safe	add -**r**: safer
Adjectives Ending in -y easy	remove the -**y** and add -**ier**: easier
Long Adjectives interesting	put **more** before the adjective: more interesting
Irregular Adjectives good bad	 better worse

- We use comparative adjectives to compare one thing with another. We use the **verb to be** + **a comparative adjective** + **than**.
  Daniel is taller than his father.

Superlatives

Superlatives	
Short Adjectives smart	add -**est**: smartest
Short Adjectives Ending in Vowel + Consonant big	double the final consonant and add -**est**: biggest
Adjectives Ending in -e safe	add -**est**: safest
Adjectives Ending in -y easy	remove the -**y** and add -**iest**: easiest
Long Adjectives interesting	put **most** before the adjective: most interesting
Irregular Adjectives good bad	 best worst

- We use superlative adjectives to say a thing or person has the most of a particular quality. We use **the** with a **superlative adjective**.
  Daniel is the tallest person in his family.

GRAMMAR PRACTICE

Comparatives

1 Match the adjectives with their opposites.

1 big `d`   a unhealthy
2 boring ☐   b short
3 easy ☐   c new
4 tall ☐   d small
5 old ☐   e difficult
6 healthy ☐   f interesting

2 Write the comparative form of the adjectives in the box next to the comparative with the same spelling rule.

> bad   comfortable   heavy   nice   old   thin

1 smarter _____ older
2 bigger _____
3 safer _____
4 easier _____
5 more interesting _____
6 better _____

3 Write sentences with comparatives about Amy's family.

1 my sister / short / me
  My sister is shorter than me.

2 my brother / young / me
  _____
  _____

3 my sister / funny / my brother
  _____
  _____

4 my mom / thin / my dad
  _____
  _____

5 my brother / old / my sister
  _____
  _____

6 my / cousin / intelligent / me
  _____
  _____

Superlatives

4 Complete the chart with the superlative.

Adjective	Comparative	Superlative
high	higher	1 _____ the highest
amazing	more amazing	2 _____
easy	easier	3 _____
bad	worse	4 _____
popular	more popular	5 _____
big	bigger	6 _____

5 Complete the sentences with the superlative form of the adjectives in parentheses.

1 I think my dad is the _____ best _____ (good) dad in the world.

2 Many soccer players are the _____ (rich) people in sports.

3 My mom says Formula 1 racing is the _____ (fast) sport.

4 This is the _____ (heavy) bag in the world! What do you have in it?

5 I think hockey is one of the _____ (dangerous) sports.

6 Which is the _____ (easy) sport to learn?

6 Complete the text with the comparative or superlative form of the adjectives in parentheses.

On Saturdays, I usually go and see my cousin play soccer. She's [1] _____ the best _____ (good) player on the team. She always scores [2] _____ (amazing) goals! She's [3] _____ (tall) player on the team, and she's [4] _____ (fast) than the others. I think she's also [5] _____ (intelligent) than her teammates because she watches what is happening all the time! She's also [6] _____ (popular) player on the team!

Simple Past: *To Be*

Affirmative		Negative	
I / He / She / It	was good.	I / He / She / It	wasn't good.
You / We / They	were good.	You / We / They	weren't good.

Questions	Short Answers	
	Affirmative	Negative
Was I / he / she / it good?	Yes, I / he / she / it was.	No, I / he / she / it wasn't.
Were you / we / they good?	Yes, you / we / they were.	No, you / we / they weren't.

- **Was** and **were** are the simple past forms of **to be**.
  There was a special gorilla in the Barcelona zoo.
  The elephants were born without tusks.

- To form questions, we use **was/were**. We don't use **do**.
  Was he a white tiger? (NOT Does he was a white tiger?)
  Were the elephants enormous?

- We form information questions with the **Wh-** question before **was/were**.
  What was it?   Where were you last night?

There Was/Were

	Affirmative	Negative
Singular	There was a gorilla at the zoo.	There wasn't a gorilla at the zoo.
Plural	There were three lions.	There weren't three lions.
Questions	Short Answers	
	Affirmative	Negative
Was there a gorilla at the zoo?	Yes, there was.	No, there wasn't.
Were there three lions?	Yes, there were.	No, there weren't.

- **There was/were** are the simple past forms of **there is/are**.
  There was a park here.   There were two cars.

- We use **there was** with singular countable nouns and uncountable nouns.
  There was a pen here.   There was some milk in the fridge.

- We use **there were** with plural countable nouns.
  There were a lot of tourists in our town last weekend.

- In questions and negatives, we usually use **any** with plural countable and uncountable nouns
  Were there any interesting animals at the zoo?
  Was there any bread at home?
  There weren't any cats.   There wasn't any rice.

Simple Past: Regular and Irregular Verbs

- We use the simple past to talk about completed events and actions in the past.
  I played basketball yesterday.
  He lived in Boston last year.

Spelling

Most Verbs	add -*ed*: *show – showed*
Verbs Ending in -*e*	add -*d*: *live – lived*
Verbs Ending in Consonant + -*y*	remove the -*y* and add -*ied*: *study – studied*
Verbs Ending in Consonant + Vowel + Consonant	double the final consonant and add -*ed*: *shop – shopped* *stop – stopped*

Irregular Verbs

- Irregular simple past verbs don't follow any pattern.
  get – got   do – did   see – saw   have – had

Simple Past: Negative

	Didn't	Infinitive	Other Words
I / You / He / She / It / You / We / They	didn't	play	soccer yesterday.
		go	to the movies.

- To form the simple past negative, we use **subject + didn't + infinitive**.
  Javier didn't watch TV last night.
  They didn't have lunch at home today.

- We can use time expressions such as **yesterday**, **last night**, **last weekend**, and **last summer** with the simple past. We usually put them at the end of a sentence.
  We went to a safari park last weekend.

- We use **ago** with the simple past to talk about when something happened. We usually put it at the end of a sentence.
  Alex arrived home two hours ago.

Simple Past: *To Be*

1 (Circle) the correct options.

1 The monkey (was) / *were* in a tree at the zoo.
2 The baby elephant *was* / *were* beautiful!
3 The bears *wasn't* / *weren't* very big, but the lions *was* / *were* enormous!
4 It *wasn't* / *weren't* a very interesting documentary – it *was* / *were* very boring!
5 We *was* / *were* at the zoo for hours!
6 Lalo *was* / *were* happy, but Emilia *wasn't* / *weren't*!

2 Put the words in the correct order to make questions. Then complete the answers with *was* or *were*.

1 happy / Lisa / was / ?
A: Was Lisa happy?
B: Yes, she ___was___ .

2 yesterday / were / Where / you / ?
A: _____
B: I _____ at home.

3 were / Who / with / you / ?
A: _____
B: My friend _____ at home with me.

4 the / zoo / Was / big / ?
A: _____
B: Yes, it _____ enormous!

5 most / What / animal / was / the / interesting / ?
A: _____
B: The tigers! They _____ beautiful.

There Was/Were

3 (Circle) the correct options.

For many years, [1]*there wasn't* / (*there weren't*) many people in my town, and [2]*there wasn't* / *there weren't* a place to see animals, but in 2015, everything changed – [3]*there was* / *there were* houses, people, children, and stores, and [4]*there was* / *there were* a new animal park! [5]*There wasn't* / *There weren't* any big animals, like elephants, but [6]*there was* / *there were* cute little animals, like rabbits and a lot of different birds. Now, it's my favorite place!

Simple Past: Regular and Irregular Verbs

4 Write the simple past form of the verbs in the chart.

Regular	watch	live	hate
	[1] watched	[5]	[9]
	plan	stop	study
	[2]	[6]	[10]
Irregular	do	eat	get
	[3]	[7]	[11]
	go	have	see
	[4]	[8]	[12]

5 Complete the text with the simple past form of the verbs in parentheses.

We [1] _arrived_ (arrive) at the animal park in the morning. My little sister [2] _____ (want) to see the birds, but they were at the other end of the park. She [3] _____ (cry) for a few minutes. Then I [4] _____ (show) her the rabbits. She [5] _____ (love) them! She [6] _____ (play) with them for hours!

6 Write the words in the correct order to make sentences.

1 week / my / went / to / dad / mountains / Last / I / the / with
Last week, I went to the mountains with my dad.

2 brown / bears / saw / big / We / two
_____

3 so / we / had / My / dad / a sandwich / was / hungry,
_____

4 behind / I / bear / me / heard / a
_____

5 up / a / tree, / I / went / bear / ate / my / sandwich / and / the
_____

6 My / the / ran / to / car / eat / his / sandwich, but / dad / didn't
_____

Simple Past: Questions

Did	Subject	Infinitive	Short Answers	
			Affirmative	**Negative**
Did	I / you / he / she / it / we / you / they	play?	Yes, I / you / he / she / it / we / you / they did.	No, I / you / he / she / it / we / you / they didn't.

- We make simple past questions with **Did** + **subject** + **the infinitive**.
  Did she enjoy the yoga class?

Simple Past: *Wh-* Questions

Question Word	Did	Subject	Verb	Other Words
Who				with?
What time				?
Where	did	I / you / he / she / it / we / you / they	go	?
What				for?
When				?
How				?

- We form **Wh-** questions in the simple past with a **question word** + **did** + **subject** + **the infinitive**.
  What time did you go to bed?
  Where did they go on vacation?
  What did you do on the weekend?
  Who did she see there?
  How did he feel?
  When did you arrive?

GRAMMAR PRACTICE

Simple Past: Questions

1 Match questions 1–5 with answers a–e.

1 Did you go to the post office this morning? [d]
2 Did you and Antonia watch TV last night? ☐
3 Did the store close early yesterday? ☐
4 Did your friends go to the bowling alley with you? ☐
5 Did our English teacher correct our homework? ☐

a No, she didn't.   d ~~Yes, I did.~~
b Yes, we did.   e No, it didn't.
c Yes, they did.

2 Look at the information about the activities Sergio and Andrea did on the weekend. Write short answers.

	Go Bowling	Clean Bedroom	Visit Grandparents	Go Swimming
Sergio	✓	✗	✓	✗
Andrea	✗	✓	✓	✗

1 Did Sergio go bowling?   Yes, he did.
2 Did Sergio clean his bedroom?   _____
3 Did Andrea clean her bedroom?   _____
4 Did Sergio visit his grandparents? _____
5 Did Andrea go swimming?   _____
6 Did Sergio go swimming?   _____

3 Write questions and short answers.

1 your cousins / see / the fish / at the / aquarium ✓
   A: *Did your cousins see the fish at the aquarium?*
   B: *Yes, they did.*

2 Daniel / go to / the skate park / yesterday ✗
   A: _____
   B: _____

3 you and Melody / meet / at the movies / today ✓
   A: _____
   B: _____

4 Olga / do / judo / last year ✗
   A: _____
   B: _____

5 you / stay / at the hospital / for a long time ✓
   A: _____
   B: _____

Simple Past: Wh- Questions

4 (Circle) the correct options.

1 A: (What)/ Where did you do on the weekend?
   B: I stayed at home.
2 A: Where / When did they play handball on Sunday?
   B: At the gym.
3 A: What / Who did he see at the ice rink?
   B: Nobody he knew.
4 A: How / When did he feel?
   B: Not very well.
5 A: How / What time did they leave?
   B: About 5 p.m.
6 A: When / Who did they catch the train?
   B: Early this morning.

5 Complete the conversation with Wh- question words from Exercise 4.

Eduardo: I like your phone. [1] _Where_ did you get it?

Ali: It's from the new shopping mall.

Eduardo: Was it expensive?

Ali: I don't know! It was a present.

Eduardo: [2] _____ bought it for you?

Ali: My mom. She got it for my birthday!

Eduardo: Wow, that's a fantastic present! [3] _____ did she get it?

Ali: She got it last week when we went shopping, but I didn't see her buy it!

Eduardo: [4] _____ did you feel when you got it?

Ali: Surprised and happy!

Eduardo: [5] _____ did I get you? I can't remember!

Ali: Nothing, you forgot!

Eduardo: Sorry!

Future with *Will/Won't*

Affirmative		Negative		Questions		Short Answers	
						Affirmative	**Negative**
I/You/He/She/It/We /You/They	will pass the exam.	I/You/He/She/It/We /You/They	won't pass the exam.	Will I/you/he/she/it/we/you/they	pass the exam?	Yes, I/you/he/she/it/we/you/they will.	No, I/you/he/she/it/we/you/they won't.

- We use **will** and **won't** to make predictions about the future.
  Computers will control our lives in the future.

- **Will/Won't** doesn't change in the third person.

- We change the word order when we form questions. We don't use **do/does**.
  Will we travel in cars in the future?

- In informal English, we use the contraction **'ll**.
  They'll sleep in a camper on vacation.

Present Continuous for Future

- We can use the present continuous to talk about fixed arrangements in the future.
  I'm meeting my friend Maite at 6:30.
  My sister's traveling to Brazil in October.

- We often use future time expressions such as **tonight**, **tomorrow**, **this weekend**, **this summer**, **next week**, **next month**, and **after class/school**.
  What are you doing tonight?
  We're traveling to Paris this summer.
  Is he coming to the party on Saturday?

Be Going To

Affirmative		Negative	
I'm		I'm not	
You're		You aren't	
He's		He isn't	
She's	going to run.	She isn't	going to run.
It's		It isn't	
We're		We aren't	
You're		You aren't	
They're		They aren't	

- We use **to be going to** to talk about future plans and intentions.

She's going to take her camera on vacation.
I'm going to wear my new sneakers.

- To form the affirmative, we use **verb to be** + **going to** + **infinitive**.
  We're going to have dinner in a restaurant.

- To form the negative, we use **verb to be** + **not** + **going to** + **verb infinitive**. **Not** is usually contracted.
  They aren't going to go on vacation this summer.

Questions	Short Answers	
	Affirmative	**Negative**
Am I going to be there?	Yes, I am.	No, I'm not.
Are you going to be there?	Yes, you are.	No, you aren't.
Is he going to be there?	Yes, he is.	No, he isn't.
Is she going to be there?	Yes, she is.	No, she isn't.
Is it going to be there?	Yes, it is.	No, it isn't.
Are we going to be there?	Yes, we are.	No, we aren't.
Are you going to be there?	Yes, you are.	No, you aren't.
Are they going to be there?	Yes, they are.	No, they aren't.

- We form questions with **verb to be** before the subject.
  Is he going to tell us the answers to the homework?

- We form information questions with a **Wh-** question word before **verb to be**.
  Who is he going to ask?
  What are you going to wear to the party?
  Why is Susana going to be late?

Future with *Will/Won't*

1 **Complete the sentences about a camping trip. Write *'ll* or *won't*.**

1 Don't sit at the bottom of the boat. You 'll _____ get wet.

2 Don't make the shelter. You _____ know how to do it.

3 Don't swim in the river. It's dangerous, so you _____ be safe!

4 Don't eat and then swim. You _____ feel sick!

5 Don't walk alone at night because you _____ get lost!

6 Don't lose your compass. You _____ know how to get back to the camp.

2 **Write sentences with *will* or *won't* about the things you can do on vacation.**

1 have a good time ✓   I will have a good time. _____

2 get bored ✗   _____

3 go to the beach every day ✓   _____

4 stay in a tent ✗   _____

5 eat good food ✓   _____

6 do any homework ✗   _____

Present Continuous for Future

3 **Complete the email with the present continuous form of the verbs in parentheses.**

Hi Sandra,

How are you? It's summer break next week! I ¹ *'m going* (go) on an adventure trip, and my sister ² _____ (come), too! In August, my dad ³ _____ (take) me on a boat trip! My mom ⁴ _____ (not go) because she doesn't like boats! She ⁵ _____ (visit) my grandparents. I think you ⁶ _____ (fly) to England for a week. Is that right? What are you doing after that?

Jorge

4 **Complete the sentences with the present continuous form of the verbs in the box.**

| come   go   have   ~~meet~~   not visit   play |

1 I'm _____ meeting _____ my friends tomorrow morning.

2 When _____ you _____ basketball?

3 _____ grandpa _____ to visit on Sunday?

4 _____ Ben and Sam _____ a party next week?

5 We _____ my aunt and uncle this weekend.

6 Where _____ you _____ shopping on Friday?

Be Going To

5 **Rewrite the sentences in the negative.**

1 I'm going to see my grandma next week.

I'm not going to see my grandma next week.

2 You are going to make new friends.

_____

3 Marina is going to visit the wildlife park next month.

_____

4 Sam is going to go to a summer camp next year.

_____

5 We are going to learn how to make a shelter.

_____

6 They are going to climb the mountain.

_____

6 **Complete the conversations with the correct form of *be going to*. Use the verbs in parentheses.**

1 **A:** *What are you going to do* _____ (do) on summer break?

B: I _____ (visit) my aunt in Chicago.

2 **A:** _____ (he / stay) in a hotel?

B: No, he _____ .

3 **A:** _____ (Gabriel and Ana / go) rock climbing in the mountains?

B: Yes, they _____ .

4 **A:** We _____ (not go) on vacation this year.

B: _____ (you / stay) at home?

LANGUAGE BANK

STARTER

Vocabulary
Months

> January   February   March   April   May
> June   July   August   September
> October   November   December

Cardinal Numbers

> one   two   three   four   five
> six   seven   eight   nine   ten

Ordinal Numbers

> first   second   third   fourth   fifth   sixth
> seventh   eighth   ninth   tenth

Colors

> black   blue   green   orange   pink
> red   yellow   white

Classroom Objects

> board   calculator   chair   dictionary
> door   notebook   pen   pencil   poster
> ruler   table   window

Grammar in Action
Subject Pronouns and
Possessive Adjectives
Verb *To Be*
Question Words
Whose + Possessive Pronouns
Imperatives

Writing
Useful Language
An Informal Letter
To start: Dear + Mr. (*man*) or Mrs./Ms. (*woman*)
+ person's surname
To end: Best wishes, Sincerely
To join two ideas in one sentence: and

UNIT 1

Vocabulary
Family Members

> aunt   brother   cousin   dad   daughter
> granddaughter   grandma
> grandpa   grandson   husband   mom
> nephew   niece   sister   son   uncle   wife

Describing People
Eyes: brown, gray
Hairstyle: long, short, wavy
Hair Color: blond, brown, gray, red
Height: short, tall
Other features: beard, freckles, glasses, mustache

Grammar in Action
To Have: Affirmative and Negative
how many … ?
Possessive *'s*

Speaking
Everyday English
Are you alright?
Cool!
Gotta go!
That's funny!
That's so not funny!

Useful Language
Bye!
Hey, (Evan).
How's it going?
OK/Fine, thanks. You?
See you later.

Writing
Useful Language
An Informal Email
At the beginning: Hi, Hey, Hello
At the end: Email me soon, That's all for now,
Write soon!
Contractions: I'm, He's, She's, We're, Here's, Who's
Symbols: use emojis to help express your feelings

LANGUAGE BANK

UNIT 2

Vocabulary
Daily Routines

> brush your teeth   check your phone
> do your homework   get dressed   get up
> go home   go to bed   go to school
> have breakfast   pack your bag
> take a shower   wake up

Free-Time Activities

> chat online   download songs   go for a bike ride
> go shopping   hang out with friends
> listen to music   make videos
> play an instrument   play video games
> read a book/magazine   take photos   watch TV

Grammar in Action
Simple Present: Affirmative and Negative
Adverbs of Frequency
Simple Present: Questions
Wh- Questions

Speaking
Everyday English
Go ahead.
It depends.
No problem.
Sure.
That's easy!

Useful Language
Is that OK?
Thank you very much for your time.
I just have some questions to ask you.
I just have one more question.
That's interesting.

Writing
Useful Language
An article
apostrophe '   exclamation point !
comma ,   period .
capital letter **A**, **B**, **C**   question mark ?

UNIT 3

Vocabulary
School Subjects

> art   drama   English   geography
> information technology (IT)   math   music
> nutrition   physical education (PE)   science
> Spanish   vocational education

Places in a School

> athletic field   auditorium   cafeteria
> classroom   computer lab   gymnasium
> library   locker room   office   restrooms
> science lab   teacher's lounge

Grammar in Action
Can for Ability and Permission
Verb Forms: (*Don't*) *Like*, *Don't Mind*, *Love*, *Hate* + *-ing*
Object Pronouns

Speaking
Everyday English
Don't be silly!
I'm stuck.
Not again!
Not great.
Oh, dear!

Useful Language
Are you sure?
Can you do me a favor?
Can you help me, please?
Do you need a hand with … ?

Writing
Useful Language
A Description
for example
like
such as

LANGUAGE BANK

UNIT 4

Vocabulary
Food and Drink

> apples   bananas   beans   carrots   cheese
> chicken   chocolate   eggs   fish
> juice   meat   rice   soda   water

Adjectives

> cold   delicious   disgusting   fresh   healthy
> hot   salty   spicy   sweet   unhealthy

Grammar in Action
Countable and Uncountable Nouns
A/An, *Some/Any*
There Is/Isn't, There Are/Aren't
Much, Many, A Lot Of

Speaking
Everyday English
Enjoy!
Here you go.
No problem.
No worries.

Useful Language
Can I have … ?
Can I help you?
How much is that?
I'd like a/an/some …
Is that everything?
That's … , please.
What kind?
What's in the … ?

Writing
Useful Language
A Description
We use *and* to add similar information.
We use *but* to contrast different information.
We use *or* when there is a choice (usually between two things).

UNIT 5

Vocabulary
Clothes

> boots   cap   flip-flops   hoodie   jacket
> jeans   shirt   shorts
> skirt   sneakers   sweatpants   T-shirt

Accessories

> belt   bracelet   earrings   gloves   necklace
> purse   ring   scarf   sunglasses   umbrella
> wallet   watch

Grammar in Action
Present Continuous
Simple Present and Present Continuous

Speaking
Everyday English
It's a bargain.
It's perfect.
No, honestly.
You're in luck!

Useful Language
Can I help you?
Can I see the … one, please?
Do you have it in a different (size/color/style)?
How about this one / these?
I'm looking for …
It comes in …

Writing
Useful Language
A Description of a Photo
in the back
in the middle
on the left/right
next to (someone)

LANGUAGE BANK

UNIT 6

Vocabulary
Sports

> basketball   football   gymnastics
> hockey   rock climbing   rugby   running
> sailing   swimming   table tennis
> track and field   volleyball   windsurfing   yoga

Sports Verbs

> bounce   catch   climb   dive   hit   jump
> kick   lift   pass   run   score   throw

Grammar in Action
Comparatives
Superlatives

Speaking
Everyday English
Got them!
Look!
That's crazy!
What are we waiting for?
Why not?

Useful Language
Do you want to go?
How much are the tickets?
Let's buy them.
Let's go.
They're ($145).
What's the (quickest/best/cheapest) way to get there?

Writing
Useful Language
A Profile of an Athlete
We use *also* and *too* to give extra information.
We use *also* after the verb *to be*.
We use *also* before other verbs.
We use *too* at the end of a sentence.
We use a comma before *too*.

UNIT 7

Vocabulary
Animals

> **Birds:**
> duck   eagle   parrot
> **Mammals:**
> bear   donkey   giraffe   hippo   horse
> lion   monkey   mouse   whale
> **Reptiles:**
> crocodile   snake

Adjectives

> beautiful   cute   dangerous   heavy
> huge   large   lazy   light   long   noisy
> quiet   safe   short   smart   tiny   wild

Grammar in Action
Simple Past: *To Be, There Was/Were*
Simple Past: Regular and Irregular Verbs

Speaking
Everyday English
No way!
Really?
Wow!
You're joking!

Useful Language
How was (the field trip)?
It was (really cool).
What about (lions)?
What was (it) like?

Writing
Useful Language
An Article
In 2017
On October 10, 2015
Several years ago

LANGUAGE BANK

UNIT 8

Vocabulary
Places in Town

> aquarium   bowling alley   gym   hospital
> ice rink   movie theater   parking lot
> post office   shopping mall   skate park
> swimming pool

Personal Possessions

> bus pass   camera   concert ticket   headphones
> ID card   keys   laptop   money   passport
> phone   portable charger   tablet

Grammar in Action
Simple Past: Questions
Simple Past: *Wh-* Questions

Speaking
Everyday English
Calm down.
Don't panic!
Gross!
Let's think.

Useful Language
Did you have it when you (got to school)?
Did you put it (in your bag)?
What did you do with it after that?
When did you last (have/use/see) it?

Writing
Useful Language
A Blog Post
I didn't hear my alarm, **so** I got up late.

UNIT 9

Vocabulary
Outdoor Life

> build a shelter   catch fish   collect wood
> cook over a campfire   find food and water
> identify plants   light a fire   pick fruit
> read a map   use a compass

Vacations

> apartment   (beach/ski) resort
> B&B (bed & breakfast)   cabin   camper   hotel
> RV (recreational vehicle)   tent   youth hostel

Grammar in Action
Future with *Will/Won't*
Present Continuous for Future
Be Going To

Speaking
Everyday English
Easy!
Forget that.
I'm on it!
You're unbelievable!

Useful Language
How about a (movie night)?
I'm not sure about that.
I'd rather not do that.
Let's do that!
What are we going to do?
Why don't we (have a picnic)?

Writing
Useful Language
An Email
at home
in August
in the morning
on Monday
on August 3
at the airport

IRREGULAR VERBS

Infinitive	Simple Past
be	was/were
beat	beat
become	became
begin	began
break	broke
bring	brought
build	built
buy	bought
catch	caught
choose	chose
come	came
cost	cost
cut	cut
do	did
draw	drew
drink	drank
drive	drove
eat	ate
fall	fell
feel	felt
fight	fought
find	found
fly	flew
forget	forgot
get	got
give	gave
go	went
grow	grew
have	had
hear	heard
hide	hid
hit	hit
hold	held
keep	kept

Infinitive	Simple Past
know	knew
leave	left
lose	lost
make	made
meet	met
pay	paid
put	put
read	read
ride	rode
ring	rang
run	ran
say	said
see	saw
sell	sold
send	sent
show	showed
shut	shut
sing	sang
sit	sat
sleep	slept
speak	spoke
spend	spent
stand	stood
swim	swam
take	took
teach	taught
tell	told
think	thought
throw	threw
understand	understood
wake	woke
wear	wore
win	won
write	wrote

ACKNOWLEDGEMENTS

The authors and publishers acknowledge the following sources of copyright material and are grateful for the permissions granted. While every effort has been made, it has not always been possible to identify the sources of all the material used, or to trace all copyright holders. If any omissions are brought to our notice, we will be happy to include the appropriate acknowledgements on reprinting and in the next update to the digital edition, as applicable.

Key: **SU** = Starter Unit, **U** = Unit

Photography

The following photographs are sourced from Getty Images.

U1: Radius Images; kali9/iStock/Getty Images Plus; Carol Yepes/Moment; Classen Rafael/EyeEm; s-cphoto/E+; scibak/iStock/Getty Images Plus; RinoCdZ/iStock/Getty Images Plus; C Squared Studios/Photodisc; AigarsR/iStock/Getty Images Plus; abell7302/iStock/Getty Images Plus; Westend61; m-imagephotography; Tempura/iStock/Getty Images Plus; Rafael Elias/Moment; SSC/Stone; Xose Casal Photography/Moment; Jose Luis Pelaez Inc/Blend Images; Gustavo Di Mario/The Image Bank; Anders Johansson/EyeEm; Floresco Productions/Cultura; Andrew Bret Wallis/The Image Bank; jane/iStock/Getty Images Plus; Thomas Barwick/Taxi; Bruce Laurance/The Image Bank; aimintang/iStock/Getty Images Plus; Kalle Singer; Juanmonino/iStock/Getty Images Plus; ImagesBazaar; Simon D. Warren/Corbis/VCG; **U2:** bamby-bhamby/iStock/Getty Images Plus; Klaus Vedfelt/DigitalVision; JGI/Jamie Grill/Blend Images; instamatic/iStock/Getty Images Plus; SolStock/iStock/Getty Images Plus; SolStock/E+; Jim Jordan Photography/The Image Bank; James Collins/Corbis; Steve Debenport/E+; Glenda Christina/Perspectives; FatCamera/E+; Lobro78/iStock/Getty Images Plus; Westend61; Purestock; Robert Daly/Caiaimage; Morsa Images/DigitalVision; Jamie Grill/The Image Bank; JGI/Tom Grill/Blend Images; Juanmonino/iStock/Getty Images Plus; Nick David/Taxi/Getty Images Plus; **U3:** Jupiterimages/Stockbyte; YinYang/E+; Wavebreakmedia/iStock/Getty Images Plus; NikolayN/iStock/Getty Images Plus; uptonpark/iStock/Getty Images Plus; Klaus Vedfelt/Taxi; Jon Feingersh/Blend Images; Mint Images RF; Eri Morita/The Image Bank; Vanda9/iStock/Getty Images Plus; Compassionate Eye Foundation/London, United Kingdom; hartcreations/E+; Image Source; Dinodia Photo/Passage; Amos Morgan/Photodisc; alongoldsmith/RooM; B2M Productions/Photographer's Choice RF; **U4:** Dougal Waters/DigitalVision; Theerawan Bangpran/iStock/Getty Images Plus; Derkien/iStock/Getty Images Plus; Magone/iStock/Getty Images Plus; rimglow/iStock/Getty Images Plus; Foodcollection RF; tc397/iStock/Getty Images Plus; MielPhotos2008/iStock/Getty Images Plus; vanillaechoes/iStock/Getty Images Plus; chengyuzheng/iStock/Getty Images Plus; ddukang/iStock/Getty Images Plus; Onegin/iStock/Getty Images Plus; Bartosz Luczak/iStock/Getty Images Plus; Astrakan Images/Cultura; imtmphoto/iStock/Getty Images Plus; Vladimir Godnik; Donald Iain Smith/Blend Images; Buena Vista Images/DigitalVision; Veronika Lipar/EyeEm; Axel Bueckert/EyeEm; Karly Pope/Moment Open; Arx0nt/iStock/Getty Images Plus; LauriPatterson/E+; Teen00000/iStock/Getty Images Plus; Science Photo Library; IvanMikhaylov/iStock/Getty Images Plus; Simone_Capozzi/iStock/Getty Images Plus; joakimbkk/iStock/Getty Images Plus; Inmagineasia; **U5:** OxfordSquare/iStock/Getty Images Plus; s-cphoto/iStock/Getty Images Plus; primeimages/E+; mfto/iStock/Getty Images Plus; mawielobob/iStock/Getty Images Plus; akova/iStock/Getty Images Plus; traveler1116/iStock/Getty Images Plus; Bounce/Cultura; 3alexd/E+; macroworld/iStock/Getty Images Plus; Maskot; gradyreese/E+; FatCamera/iStock/Getty Images Plus; Richard Drury/DigitalVision; Jeremy Woodhouse/Blend Images; **U6:** omgimages/iStock/Getty Images Plus; FrankRamspott/iStock/Getty Images Plus; Sam Kadiri/EyeEm; Hermann Erber/LOOK-foto; Meinzahn/iStock/Getty Images Plus; bowdenimages/iStock/Getty Images Plus; Cultura Exclusive/Rebecca Nelson; David Rogers/Getty Images Sport; Patrik Giardino/Corbis; gbh007/iStock/Getty Images Plus; Erik Isakson/Blend Images; Will Gray/AWL Images; Dennis Grombkowski/Getty Images Sport; Ramin Burhani/EyeEm; Echo/Juice Images; Foto Olimpik/NurPhoto; Feng Li/Getty Images Sport; Markus Gann/EyeEm; Hero Images; Ty Allison/Photographer's Choice; lzf/iStock/Getty Images Plus; Tim Clayton - Corbis/Corbis Sport; skynesher/E+; **U7:** Dugwy/iStock/Getty Images Plus; GlobalP/iStock/Getty Images Plus; mtruchon/iStock/Getty Images Plus; Alexey_Seafarer/iStock/Getty Images Plus; reisegraf/iStock/Getty Images Plus; PAUL J. RICHARDS/AFP; Chasing Light - Photography by James Stone james-stone.com/Moment; ROGER HARRIS/Science Photo Library; CoreyFord/iStock/Getty Images Plus; kavram/iStock/Getty Images Plus; SharafMaksumov/iStock/Getty Images Plus; Jim Cumming/Moment; Sudowoodo/iStock/Getty Images Plus; MariaArefyeva/iStock/Getty Images Plus; Quim Roser/Cultura; COffe72/iStock/Getty Images Plus; PeopleImages/E+; Sean Fleming/EyeEm; CreativeNature_nl/iStock/Getty Images Plus; Mostafa Gabr/EyeEm; ERNESTO BENAVIDES/AFP; Barrie Thomas/EyeEm; Dave Fleetham/Design Pics/Perspectives; Anup Shah/Stockbyte; Dennis George Booth/EyeEm; Paul A. Souders/Corbis Documentary; Jeffrey Coolidge/DigitalVision; Janos/iStock/Getty Images Plus; Tim Platt/Stone; Danita Delimont/Gallo Images; baronvsp/iStock/Getty Images Plus; Mr_Khan/iStock/Getty Images Plus; jashlock/iStock/Getty Images Plus; **U8:** fotovampir/iStock/Getty Images Plus; lkpgfoto/iStock/Getty Images Plus; GOLFX/iStock/Getty Images Plus; Colin Anderson Productions pty ltd/DigitalVision; MandM_Photo/iStock/Getty Images Plus; Chalabala/iStock/Getty Images Plus; Weekend Images Inc/E+; PhotoAlto/Odilon Dimier/PhotoAlto Agency RF Collections; Fancy/Veer/Corbis; bbostjan/E+; Westend61; farakos/iStock/Getty Images Plus; urbancow/E+; PBNJ Productions/Blend Images; Steve Woods Photography/Cultura; duncan1890/DigitalVision Vectors; gresei/iStock/Getty Images Plus; luismmolina/iStock/Getty Images Plus; Creative Crop/DigitalVision; rustemgurler/iStock/Getty Images Plus; Jamie Grill; Michael Burrell/iStock/Getty Images Plus; cudger/iStock/Getty Images Plus; Cahir Davitt/AWL Images; Ingolf Hatz/Cultura; Maremagnum/Photodisc; Ed Bock/Corbis; Jon Shireman/Photonica; Spaces Images/Blend Images; wakila/E+; ihoe/iStock/Getty Images Plus; kevinjeon00/E+; Vostok/Moment & Vostok/Moment; Perboge/iStock Editorial/Getty Images Plus; **U9:** Daft_Lion_Studio/iStock/Getty Images Plus; Zero Creatives/Cultura; GomezDavid/E+; Westend61; PeopleImages/E+; Don Mason/Blend Images; Ryan McVay/Photodisc; ewg3D/iStock/Getty Images Plus; jfoltyn/iStock/Getty Images Plus.

The following photographs are sourced from other library.

SU, U1, U3, U5, U8 & U9: Carboxylase/Shutterstock.

Illustration

SU, U3, U5, U6: Antonio Cuesta; **U1, U4, U5:** Jose Rubio; **U1, U5, U6:** Alex Herrerias.

Cover design and illustrations: Collaborate Agency

Audio Recordings: Eastern Sky Studios

American English Consultant: Cara Norris-Ramirez

Freelance Editors: Sue Costello, Suzanne Harris, Rebecca Raynes, and Gareth Vaughan